MOVING THROUGH WALLS

MOVING
THROUGH
WALLS

THE FOUR FOUNDATIONS TO
LIVING YOUR BEST LIFE

ISRAEL
ELLIS

www.movingthroughwalls.com

Publisher: MTW Press
Editor: Kathryn Willms

Issued in print and electronic formats.
ISBN 978-1-9990105-0-8 (softcover).-- ISBN 978-1-9990105-1-5
(hardcover).—ISBN 978-1-9990105-2-2 (EPUB).

This is an original print edition of *Moving Through Walls*.

To Limore, my partner,
and Arielle, Eitan, Dov, and Dean.
You are the beats to my heart
and helped to heal the boy inside.

We and the world will heal
Through love and kindness
Charity and blessing
Mercy and life
And peace

If I am not for myself, who will be for me?

But if I am not for myself, what am I?

-Hillel, Ethics of the Fathers, 1:14

In memory of

Eliasz Rubinowicz

1919–2009

CONTENTS

Author's Note

This book is centered on a simple tenet: that every person has the capacity to become the greatest version of themselves. We have no control over the circumstances in which we start life—the advantages or disadvantages we are born into—but regardless of who we are, what our backgrounds are, and what we have endured, we all have the ability to access and realize our greatest selves.

How do I know this tenet to be true, and why should you trust me? I am not a certified practitioner in psychotherapy. I am not a healer by profession. I do not have advanced degrees in philosophy or psychology. I have never written a book before. However, I know we can realize our greatest selves because I've lived the journey. My credentials are the road I have traveled.

I grew up being physically and emotionally abused. My home was repressive and dysfunctional, and I was sent away at the age of 13 to religious schools that perverted my spirit. Throughout my youth, I struggled with my identity, substance abuse, self-confidence, and self-worth. I was vulnerable and preyed upon. In other words, I was the perfect example of a person destined to self-destruct.

But I didn't. I changed my destiny. I became an emotionally healthy adult who found purpose and satisfaction in my life and career. After great effort to attain an education, I moved from the darkness of my youth into the light. Today, I am a self-styled business leader, one who has founded successful companies in diverse industries. More importantly, however, I am a caring husband to my wife, and I am a father to four wonderful and amazing kids.

But this book is not about my journey; it's about yours. I wrote this book because I found purpose in sharing what I've learned. Through this book, I hope to give you a roadmap to becoming your best self. In turn, I ask you to pass along what you learn to others. Our existence is circular. Our deeds, attitudes, and energies circle back to us. So many people and their ideas have provided inspiration and aided me on my journey; I hope I can help you on yours. As the ancient Talmud wisely states: "Save one life and save the world."

In the pages that follow, you will find practices, philosophies, attitudes, and anecdotes that will challenge you to rethink your existing assumptions and your life path, before encouraging you to commit to something revolutionary. Much of what I say in this book may have been said by others, some of them philosophers or visionaries who have devoted their lives to studying these topics. I won't claim to have their level of mastery; rather, I will offer a different—more personal—perspective. Instead of philosophizing about overcoming barriers (which I call "moving through walls"), I will tell you how I have done it. I am empirical evidence of the truth and value of the ideas and practices contained in these pages.

My entire life has been about confronting the walls placed in front of me, and believing I can move through them. From a young age I refused to accept the status quo and intuitively knew that I could create the future I wanted. With this hunger, I would indeed go on to make my dreams come true. However, on a daily basis, I still confront these metaphorical walls and work to penetrate them using the four foundational principles I discuss in this book.

We all have the choice of watching walls grow and shadow our aspirations, or we can confront the walls and move through them. Once you believe that you have the power to move through any wall, there is nothing that can hold you back from achieving your greatness.

Achieving personal greatness is not just a box you tick before moving on to your next task. Becoming, and then staying at, our personal best requires continual practice, discipline, and commitment. In the same way that we exercise our bodies, we must continually work to maintain a state of mind that allows us to access our greatness—all the time!

Greatness is built upon four foundational principles. Envision for a moment an ancient shrine that you discovered after a long search; it is buried beneath wild vegetation, barely visible. You clear away the leaves and dirt and discover inscribed upon it four pillars. As you read them, you feel their impact and start to sense how they work together to provide a supporting infrastructure for all you do.

Openness, faith, future, and forgiveness. Being open to the world around us, building our sense of faith that what needs to happen will happen, being able to visualize the future we want, and forgiving ourselves and others so we can move forward. Maintaining a healthy sense of self is like nutrition for the mind; it provides us with the base we need to forge ahead and become our greatest selves.

This book is founded on the principle that all of us can enact positive change in our lives. However, before going any further, I want to express great empathy for those who suffer from mental illness and acknowledge that mental illness cannot be remedied through strength of mind alone. That said, having a mental illness does not preclude you from becoming your best self; it may just alter the path you need to take to get there. I hope and believe that each of the lessons and practices presented here will be helpful to every person who approaches them with an open mind and is willing to use these elements as a foundation for their actions and being.

Are you ready to realize the power of becoming your greatest self? Are you ready to finally answer the question of what you really want from life?

Writing this book has taken me back into the far recesses of my life. It has reminded me of where I came from, where I have been, and where I want to go. I am richer and better off for having gone through this process. I am grateful for the opportunity to share what I have learned, and I am so very grateful to you, for reading these words and taking the leap to imagine a better future where you will move through walls and achieve your greatest self.

Chapter One

LOOK UP

Everything can be taken from a man but one thing: the last of the human freedoms – to choose one's attitude in any given set of circumstances, to choose one's own way.

-*Viktor Frankl,* Man's Search for Meaning

When I was seven years old, I had an epiphany that changed the course of my life. I was a skinny, lanky kid, with mismatched socks rising over scrawny bruised legs, below ill-fitting hand-me-down canvas shorts that were held up by a string around my waist. In this uniform, I spent hot summer days trying to stay under the radar in a desperate, unhappy place. I liked to imagine turning into a bird and flying away. I can't remember if that was what I was thinking about that day as I stood in my backyard, but the notion of escape was always on my mind. Shutting my eyes tight, arching my back and lifting my face to the sun—bathing in its warmth, feeling a few brief moments of peace as its heat penetrated through me and then, unwittingly, unknowingly—quite suddenly—opening my eyes. The pain in my retinas shocked me into a sudden understanding of the insignificance of my unhappiness in the face of that big ball of fire. In that moment, I realized my life was my own, and that it could—

no, it would—be different. I alone had the ability to make it different. My life started with me. As I stood in the middle of that overgrown lawn, I made a commitment to take control of my life as soon as I possibly could. That would be my true escape.

I surely didn't know then what I know now, which is that I was seeking more than just to flee my dysfunctional childhood. Simply surviving was not the happy ending I sought; rather, what I wanted was much harder to achieve and would require a real and sustained engagement with my own desires, agency, and power.

Athletes strive for peak performance, artists for perfect beauty, and entrepreneurs for that elusive idea that will light the world on fire. At a more basic level, I believe that most people want to strive for greatness. But like water flowing downhill, pulled along by gravity, people naturally seek the path of least resistance. Indeed, it is easier to react to events than it is to take responsibility for our own path forward. It is simpler to believe that the highs and lows of life are natural and inevitable, rather than to accept the part we play in creating them.

> *I have spent periods of my life in a lowly reactive place where I am running from one problem to the next, seemingly unable to stop the onslaught. These moments, when I'm most stressed, are when I attract the worst in the world, and in turn, give the worst of myself back.*

Imagine a graph; the horizontal axis represents time. If you were to chart the level of happiness and success you feel at any given moment on the vertical axis, what would your graph look like? Most people's graph would be an extreme rollercoaster of highs and lows. The reality is that most of us expect life to look that way; we assess our quality of life by taking some sort of average, establishing and defining a middle ground where things are normal and fine. Nothing more and nothing less. As long as our graph doesn't deviate from the norms surrounding us, we are satisfied with settling for that average. In fact, sometimes it seems like average is the best we can strive for. It is easier to think of the myriad responsibilities, accountabilities, decisions, and challenges we face every day as a thousand tiny weights that are there to hold us down, rather than as a thousand opportunities to live bigger and better lives.

> *I was once caught in an undertow, and I will never forget the experience. Your basic instinct is to fight for the surface, but this is a mistake. You have to surrender, hold still, relax, and let the current itself bring you back up to the surface.*

As tempting as it is to try to shed these weights or fight against them, success comes from having faith and embracing the opportunities they provide, and then kicking like hell for the top.

Throughout history, people have overcome incredible odds to do just that. They have started in lowly places, survived extreme injustices, and then overcome incredible challenges to reach the heights of success—in both their professional and personal lives. Just to have survived their circumstances might be considered success, but they did far more than that. They achieved greatness. We hear their stories and think: *What is it that drives these people? What makes them get up every day and become their best selves? What is their secret?*

What I've come to realize is that what makes these people great exists within all of us. We all have the potential to overcome countless odds and find success. We all can be great. So what's stopping us?

First of all, there is the problem of inertia. It is far easier to live reactively than it is to take a proactive role in your life. Reactive living places events and circumstances outside of our control. It is like playing a video game; we move forward towards goals others set for us, dealing with problems as they arise. This way of life is simple because we are not in charge; we have placed the power over our lives in the hands of others.

But here's the issue. When we live reactively, we have to play with the cards we're dealt. Reactive living saps our power to create change. It limits our possibilities and creative powers. One of the greatest gifts we have is the ability to decide how we live our lives. When we exercise this privilege, we can change the things that aren't working for us, we can choose goals that get us the things we really need and desire, and in this way we can shed the chains of mediocrity to achieve happiness and fulfill our need for personal greatness.

Being reactive is a hard habit to break, and not just because of inertia. One of the major impediments to creating change in our lives is the pleasure we take in causing ourselves pain. When I was 19 years old, I remember asking myself a very simple question: *Why am I messing up my life so much?*

I found my answer in the works of Edmund Bergler. Bergler was a Freudian theorist who believed that many people experience a phenomenon he called "psychic masochism." In his 1954 text, *The Revolt of the Middle-Aged Man,* Bergler wrote, "Psychic masochism, while still largely an unknown disease, is one of the most widespread of human failings. To define it briefly, it is the unconscious wish to defeat one's conscious aims, and to enjoy that self-constructed defeat."[1] In other words, Bergler argues that we

---

[1] Bergler was riffing off Sigmund Freud (1856–1939), who saw anxieties, depression, unhappiness, and distress as unconsciously motivated negative manifestations of what he referred to as a state of neurosis. Bergler believed that as children, we have to reconcile the natural aggression we feel towards our caregivers that results from realizing we are not omnipotent with the drive

derive pleasure from the anxieties and unhappiness we experience, and that is why we keep putting ourselves in situations and behaving in ways that cause us pain, continually feeding a destructive cycle of our own making. In plain English, we derive unconscious (emotional) pleasure from our own pain.

When I discovered this idea, it was like a light bulb went on. When I openly recognized the ways in which I was creating and sustaining, and—perversely—enjoying the pain in my life, I could finally start to develop a set of actions that would ultimately change my life outcomes. I could now see my self-destructive behaviors for what they were: barriers I had constructed to prevent change and deny myself real happiness and success. I was feeding into the injustices of my young life and giving into my own ingrained feeling of inferiority. I desperately needed to break free from this vicious cycle if I was going to survive.

Deriving pleasure from pain goes hand-in-hand with reactive living. They are both ways we limit ourselves, and both explain why we struggle to enact change in our lives. Think about this the next time you are experiencing pain over something. If you dig deep enough, is it possible to find some choice that you actively made that led directly to the pain you are now experiencing? In other words: *Is there something that you could have done differently to avoid the current mess you're in?*

The next question then becomes: *Can you open yourself up to the idea that things go wrong because there is a part of you that receives pleasure from them going wrong?* This is one of the most difficult questions we can confront ourselves with: the

---

towards pleasure, and we end up solving this problem by conflating two seemingly contradictory feelings: pleasure and pain. The issue occurs when we continue this pattern into adulthood and risk becoming what he termed "injustice collectors," people who create situations to extract pleasure from the injustice that results. I will discuss this idea of injustice collectors later in the book.

idea that, in our pursuit of pleasure, we might act against our own interests.

This question actually feels counterintuitive, and many people retreat into disbelief and defensiveness when I present this concept to them. However, the sooner we overcome this aversion and come to accept this uncomfortable truth about ourselves, the sooner we can identify our triggers and move past this barrier.

As humans living in a busy world, it is, I think, a natural impulse to want to rationalize and explain away the bad things that happen in our lives. However, I have found huge power in simply having the faith to accept the link between pleasure and pain as being true. To ensure that I keep moving forward, I've created the following mantra: *When things go wrong, I am responsible. On some level, there is pleasure in the pain I am in.*

By vocalizing this statement, or one similar, when something goes wrong, you challenge your unconscious motivation and bring the absurdity of the notion of self-destruction to the surface. This recognition allows you to be conscious of the possibility that you are unconsciously motivated to make choices that result in self-destruction. This awareness can bring about results that are nothing less than stunning; somewhat autonomously the motivation for your actions will shift to create positive outcomes. The more you remind yourself of the part you play in the things that go wrong in your life, albeit on an unconscious level, the better you become at making intuitive choices that work in your favor. It is uncanny how immediate and effective this practice can become, once you put your faith and trust in it!

Finally, many of us find it difficult to change because we struggle to bridge the gap between our intentions and taking action. For example, we may say to ourselves: *I want to live healthier because I know that it will make me feel great and look good. Living healthier means eating right and working out.*

This statement is a good example of articulating an intention, but what comes next? The first night we may say "no" to dessert, but the second night we might think, *one cookie won't hurt.* Then, work gets busy and we don't find the time to make it to the gym.

Our stressors can provide an excuse to break down the intent of changing our behaviors because our actions are not grounded in a real vision for ourselves. Even when our intentions are good and well thought out, they only work for us when we turn them into meaningful action, which means breaking bad habits, forming new habits, and embracing our power to create change.

The practices described within these pages are meant to enable actions that will fulfill your intentions. This is your journey. When Columbus set sail on the Santa Maria in 1492, he did so without knowing what lay ahead of him, except for a faith that something great did. He took specific actions that enabled him to overcome significant challenges to meet his intention of undertaking his exploratory mission. Now, it's your turn to set forth into the unknown and discover your greatness.

Every journey has ups and downs—my path from that scared little kid to today definitely had its rocky moments—but it is important to remember that even when aspects of life are not within our control, it does not mean that we have to be out of control. To make this journey to enact change in your life you need to trust in yourself. Let your guiding beacon be your vision of what your life could be; your healthy intuition will act as your GPS, providing real-time guidance and course correction as you strike out into uncharted territory. To reach your destination, you will need to find a balance between competing priorities and the desire for immediate gratification.

It is important to recognize that there will be times that we may fall into the trap of wanting everything at once. However, acting in pursuit of immediate gratification can come at the cost of meeting our responsibilities and impinge upon our longer-term outlook. We need to work, but crave freedom. We are naturally selfish but (hopefully) recognize that through giving we support the people we love and our commitment to society, which ultimately serves to sustain and nurture us. We want the latitude to be creative but the structure to be supported in our creative endeavors. Only by attaining this balance between impulses can we prepare and be prepared for opportunities that arise, and ultimately set ourselves up to successfully bridge the gap between intentions and action, trusting that right things will happen at the right time.

As you read this book, I hope you will spend time thinking about your passions and purpose—i.e., what you want, what's important to you, and who you want to be. This self-reflection is the creative part of the process for achieving your greatest self. But it is only with structure, discipline, and commitment that we can find the focus and fuel to make these visions our reality. It is easy to get caught up and energized by the many ideas and possibilities that run through our minds. If I simply followed the random thoughts that entered my brain in a typical day, I would bounce all over the place like a Mexican jumping bean. However, with a degree of discipline, openness, and faith, you can focus your energy to achieve that which will serve your future.

This book looks to harness your inner chaos and provide stability, tethering, and focus. As you read, take note of each idea and every sentence that speaks to you. Don't hesitate to take a step back, close your eyes, and consciously breathe in and out. Visualize. Consider where you fit into your own ideas.

Every morning, with the awakening of a new day, we are given a wonderful gift that separates us from instinctual beings—we have the power of choice. You have the power to choose the actions you will take to honor and express thanks for this gift of life. Use this book as your guide to achieve a higher state of consciousness, to help you remove impediments that prevent the answers you seek from surfacing. These answers will allow you to become your greatest self: the best lover, the best partner, the best parent, the best friend, the best employee, the best boss, the best person. The journey starts now.

What I call the four foundations—openness, faith, future, and forgiveness—are principles that we can use to change the way we interact with the world. These foundations will be the topics of Part One of this book. Our perception—how we see the world around us—is shaped by our life experiences. In our earliest years, we form many of the biases we carry throughout our lives; these biases often predict how we react to the world around us and prevent us from making the changes necessary to living our greatest lives. But it doesn't have to be this way. We all have the potential to become mindful of our biases and loosen their grip upon us. With conscious effort, we can achieve a state of being that aligns with who we want to be, not where we came from.

People often say that change starts with altering actions and behaviors, but I believe this statement is a case of mistaking means for ends. We start the change process by having a vision of who we want to be or what we want to accomplish. Only then will our actions and behaviors change to accommodate that vision.

As you start your journey, don't put emphasis on what you need to "do" to become great. It is easy to get caught up in creating a list of best practices to becoming a better person: Do this. Don't do that. Exercise every day. Network. Don't hang out with negative people. Don't smoke. But if you don't start with a clear visualization of who you are and who you want to be, any changes in behavior or actions will remain superficial. When faced with original stressors, you can easily fall back into your same old hurtful patterns.

Achieving greatness begins with a focus on who you are and who you want to be. By visualizing this concept and putting your full belief into it, you will naturally gravitate towards behaviors and actions that will help you realize the future you seek. The four foundations of openness, faith, future, and forgiveness will help you develop a strong sense of self, clear biases and blockages that are holding you back, and act as a springboard, launching you to new heights, beyond what you could have ever imagined.

Foundation 1: Openness

Visualize yourself as an infant waking up to the wonders of the world for the first time, experiencing your first tastes, smells, and sights. In this moment—this beginning—there is openness. You have no preconceived notions of the world you have been born into. No bias, no judgment. Everything is shiny and new, and anything is possible. The reality is that we can never fully recapture this state; in our formative years, we are shaped by our communities and through these communities we develop opinions, judgments, and biases. Our experience is always subjective. But imagining a state of complete openness can be useful.

Opening up beyond our own truths and value systems can feel counterintuitive to our goal of living our best life, but in fact, it is a vital part of transcending our singular subjective existence to reach something greater. Being open requires a willingness to accept and act beyond our own bias, to dismiss all preconceived and learned notions, and to engage in the art of true listening, where we let go of what we "know" and expand our perception of the world to envelop others. The practice of openness is the gateway to achieving your destiny.

Foundation 2: Faith

Faith is not a religious idea in the context of this book. Rather faith refers to the self-belief that there is a road ahead that you are meant to walk, that you are loved, and that you have a place in the universe. And while it is important to do everything in your power to set yourself up for success, there is ultimately a power greater than yourself that will determine what that success looks like. Much of what happens in our lives is beyond our illusions of control. Faith is the door that leads to the wonderful unknown.

I personally believe in the power of faith because I've seen it in action. Looking back on my own life, there have been far too many miraculous, chance occurrences to simply dismiss them as serendipitous or rationalize them away. I've come to believe that these miraculous events weren't random; they were an alignment of my life with the universe at large and they unfolded at the exact time and place required to bring me to where I needed to be. But I had to play my part, offering up the best of myself each and every time.

When you give up the notion of control, you invite the power of faith into your life, which creates this magical momentum that pushes you forward into new opportunities and ultimately allows your destiny to unfold.

Foundation 3: Future

Once you have embraced openness and faith, you can begin to actively shape and determine your future. However, this step requires a belief in the possibilities that lie ahead. Your future is decided by the actions you take today. These actions will be influenced by past events and experiences. So, in order to take control of our future, we must first be accountable to our past and make decisions in our present that are in line with where we want to go tomorrow.

Taking control of our future requires us to examine what gives us purpose and meaning in life. If we do not know what we want, we can't take an active role in shaping our future. Ultimately, we can't control what the universe will put in front of us, and as such the future will always be in some ways unknowable. But if we know what we want to happen, we become open to the possibilities that surround us, and if we have faith that the universe will deliver what we need, we can put ourselves in a position to realize the future we desire. You have to take risks to avoid regret. Sometimes, we have to step out into the void, trusting only our faith as our guide.

In Viktor Frankl's *Man's Search for Meaning* (1946), he describes the notion of identity loss he underwent during his internment in the Auschwitz concentration camp. Frankl believed that without a clear sense of self—what he called one's "personal meaning"—we lose the very idea of a future. And when we can't fathom a future, we have nothing to look forward to; the future feels like a void, a vast, empty space.

People who experience emotional and physical abuse, especially in their formative years, often struggle to figure out who they are and where they belong; they lack "personal meaning." I struggled with this as well. After all: *How can anything mean something when your own life doesn't?* Other people I've met in both my professional and personal life have been affected by this sort of "meaninglessness" at some point of their lives.

I often refer to people who feel lost and overcome with the monotony of their existence as "Cubical Joes." These are people who accept being limited in exchange for the illusion of security, but who also often find the walls closing in, suffocating the possibilities of their futures. The answer to this monotony is not necessarily to quit your job or upend your career track, but it is important to recognize this feeling for what it is, and to find something else in your life that fulfills you and imparts that sense of meaning.

I am very concerned with what I see as a crisis emerging among our younger generations. We are now experiencing a killer drug epidemic unlike any seen in the past,[2] and are losing more and more people to drug use and suicide. It is difficult to understand this epidemic, which has touched all levels of society, especially because it has occurred in a moment of unprecedented lifestyle comforts and advantages. I recently heard from a parent who had just lost their son, someone who seemingly had everything to look forward to. *What is wrong with this picture?* When people are unable to visualize a future, they can easily fall victim to a valley of meaninglessness in their lives. They then try to fill that void in dangerous ways.

I have interviewed many people in their 20s and 30s who had an attitude that all that can be done has already been thought of and achieved. I worry that these statements signal that they too will give up too easily and not have the tools to visualize a future beyond what

---

[2] In 2017, there were an estimated 68,400 drug overdose deaths in the US, more than the annual number of deaths from AIDS at the height of that epidemic. These deaths have contributed to an overall decrease in life expectancy among middle-aged white people in the US (From: Hall W D, Farrell M. (2018). Reducing the opioid overdose death toll in North America. *PLoS Med* 15(7)).

others expect of them. It's, again, the path of least resistance, not the path to greatness. People need to answer the "want" questions in their life to satisfy the innate "need" to live a life of purpose and gratitude.

Restoring personal meaning is foundational to believing in your future, and the ability to visualize your future allows you to take the necessary actions to fulfill your intentions. These pieces form a runway that will allow you to accelerate and lift off to greatness.

> *This is your captain speaking. Buckle up for your future. We are taking off, fueled by our openness and faith, accompanied by our sense of meaning. The future is before us—clear skies ahead.*

Foundation 4: Forgiveness

The final foundation is forgiveness. When an injustice has been perpetrated against you, it can be incredibly difficult to heal and move forward. That said, when we hang on to the anger that resides deep within us, it tarnishes the soul and blurs our ability to envision and realize the future we desire. To move forward, we must prevail and overcome. But how? How do you move on?

The chapter on forgiveness was the hardest and most personal for me to write. For a long time I struggled to forgive people who had hurt me, but in my journey I realized that only through forgiveness can we unlock a future in which we become the best versions of ourselves. That future is worth the discomfort of being vulnerable.

For me, forgiveness was the antidote to all the injustices and pain I experienced in my childhood. It was a release. As long as you harbor anger and hate, you will never be able to move forward. You just won't. And if you are not able to move forward, you will have difficulty being happy and thus be unable to become your best self.

If you are now holding on to pain, forgiveness will be critical to you being able to unlock your potential. Is your desire to be the greatest version of yourself worth letting go of your hurt and pain and learning to forgive? Trust me when I tell you how important this is. Do it. Forgive. Do it for yourself. Drop that weight. You will find what once felt impossible will now be within your grasp.

These four foundations set the groundwork for achieving personal greatness. In the following pages, I avoid terms like "bettering" oneself, as this term implies a judgment of who we were and where we have been. Nothing is accomplished by beating ourselves up about our past. In fact, those past experiences are important; they are learning opportunities that led us to where we are today—which is exactly where we are meant to be.

To begin this new journey, it is important to be honest with yourself about who you are in this moment. This candor will empower you and help you answer the question of who you would like to be tomorrow. When we are aligned with the universe, we can do no wrong.

Some people refer to those who seem to make the right decisions all the time as having a "golden touch": I would argue that what is really happening is they have aligned their energies with those of the universe. By being open, by having faith, by seeing their future, and by forgiving, they have set themselves up to accept opportunities that arise. Most of us have experienced moments like this, when everything just seems to come together. It's as if all the variables suddenly synchronize. *What if that happened for you all the time? What if you possessed this golden touch every day of your life?* This ability is what I mean by the term "personal greatness."

The second half of this book focuses on putting the four foundations into practice. Confidence and purpose are necessary elements for you to be able to commit to actions that will help you realize your future. Confidence is built on self-belief, which comes first and foremost from loving yourself and feeling loved. How you feel about who you are motivates the rituals that become your actions and behaviors. Purpose is the ultimate derivation of self. It's the passion that drives your actions. When our actions align with our purpose, our needs are answered, and magic happens. Finding your life's purpose is like coming upon a path that leads you through the denseness of the forest and into the light.

With every achievement—great or small—we gain momentum; our confidence builds, our purpose is reinforced, and our future comes into focus. We have all experienced doubt at times. That's natural. But doubts and setbacks don't need to shake our faith in ourselves. Positive achievements are the fuel that powers our confidence and keeps us moving forward. I call these achievements—the topic of their own chapter—accelerators. Walls we move through, mountains we climb, milestones we achieve, people we help, careers we build, ideas we bring to life— these are all accelerators.

> *I visualize myself on a unicycle balancing on a single wheel, constantly adjusting my centripetal force, while I spin a variety of objects, each with its own momentum that must be maintained. What seems impossible becomes possible; I will it too, powered by my confidence and purpose.*

The final piece of the puzzle to achieving greatness—and the topic of the second last chapter—is self-worth. Self-worth comes from knowing and valuing ourselves. Without self-worth, we can't believe in nor realize our innate greatness. This book is about living life in the zone where the game is played to the fullest. Where you are the best and the most you can be. This journey and these philosophies and practices put me on the path to achieving my greatest self. You can walk it, too.

PART I

THE FOUR FOUNDATIONS

Chapter Two

TUNE IN

*When we least expect it, life sets us a challenge to test our
courage and willingness to change; at such a moment, there is no
point in pretending that nothing has happened or in saying that
we are not yet ready. The challenge will not wait. Life does not
look back.*

-Paulo Coelho, The Devil and Miss Prym

The journey starts with a single breath. Breathe. In this
moment, you have the choice to tune in. To open yourself up
to ideas you may have shied away from, behaviors outside your
comfort zone, and practices that have the power to change the way
you live and the world you live in.

But first, just breathe. Pull the air deep into your abdomen, and
let it surface naturally through you. Do this again. With each
breath, expel the negative thoughts and feelings that are taking up
residence in your head. Raise your arms, stretch your fingers
towards the sky, and let the tension exit your body.

Put this book down and close your eyes (no one's looking!). And
while your eyes are closed, imagine that this is the first moment of
your life, and in each moment to come, you have the choice to do
the things you want to do, and be the person you want to be.

I am free. I am capable. I am entitled to be happy and successful. I will live this gift of life to its fullest.

Imagine doing all the things you do every day, but with intent. By being mindful, we hit the reset button, bring ourselves back to our center, and refocus our energies. The topic of this chapter— openness—is an exercise in intent. It's about inviting the world and all its possibilities into your life. The governing principle is to bring yourself to the present where you can take ownership and act on your intentions.

Tuning in to the world is critical to achieving clarity. Ironically, today, even with the volume of information we are being bombarded with on a daily basis, it is easier than ever to be trapped by our preconceived notions. To deal with the onslaught of information, we fall back on what we already think to be true. But when we do this, we limit ourselves.

Opening yourself up to really listening and taking in what you hear and observe is the first step to achieving greatness. By taking this step, the world becomes a blank canvas, and a million little jars of paint are laid out before you. You can draw any vision in any color using your own signature style. By not being open, you are too busy reacting to the world around you to see all the colors and their infinite possibilities, and you risk missing the opportunity to create.

Openness is a four-stage process: openness, willingness, acceptance, and action. The first requisite is to open ourselves up to ideas and thoughts, even when they oppose our own beliefs. Next, we need to be willing to acknowledge, listen, and understand—to give other people and ideas the benefit of the doubt. People will say things that will counter our own belief system and may cause us to become defensive and emotional, sometimes to the point that we will refuse to hear them. However, we must let go of our biases and put aside our emotional responses in order to see the possibilities in what we are hearing. Finally, to put what we've learned into use, we must act. Paying close attention to the outcomes of this process will provide us with insights into how to integrate openness into our daily practice.

To achieve greatness, we must be open and ready to accept new information, even if it conflicts with our existing view of the world. In 1957, Leon Festinger coined the term "cognitive dissonance" to describe the tension and discomfort we experience when the various beliefs and ideas we have about the world conflict with each other. For example, imagine someone who is concerned about their health and takes care to buy organic food also smokes. Even if they know that smoking is one of the worst things they can do for their health, they may rationalize that their other healthy living choices make up for this poor choice.

Even companies can display cognitive dissonance. I recently walked into a trendy eco store in downtown Miami and bought one of their live juices. After drinking it, I took the bottle up to the cashier and asked her where the recycling container was. The cashier was embarrassed and visibly uncomfortable as she admitted that the company does not recycle, despite selling their products using an ethos of being responsible to the environment!

When we experience cognitive dissonance, we feel uncomfortable, and our first instinct is to try to reduce the dissonance. The most obvious way to do this is to remove inconsistencies. In the examples above, the person who cares about their health could stop smoking. The company could begin recycling. Another way to deal with dissonance is to change our beliefs to match how we "want" to behave. For example, we might look for alternative research that downplays how bad smoking is for us, or explains why recycling is not an effective way to help the environment; if it is convincing, that might encourage us to alter our belief system to match our actions.

Getting wrapped up in the political populism of the day can put people in a continual state of cognitive dissonance, where they may find themselves advocating for or against actions or causes about which they have no personal experience or direct understanding. We are all entitled to our opinions, regardless of our level of knowledge or understanding, but when we close our minds to alternative discourse, we risk entering into a state of dissonance.

Refusing to accept new information presented to us is akin to sweeping it under the rug, and also leads to cognitive dissonance. Often, our reaction may be to become defensive and to attempt to justify our point of view while invalidating what we have just learned. Even though we know better, we try to deny reality in favor of maintaining our preconceived notions. This defensiveness is an emotional response that exerts control over us, and is in turn reflected in our actions.

The powerful impulse to maintain cognitive consistency can result in irrational and maladaptive behaviors. It can also stifle our creativity, especially when we close ourselves off to new ideas. Furthermore, being in a state of cognitive dissonance depletes our sense of self-worth.

To avoid the negative effects of cognitive dissonance, we must confront it head on. It is only when we bring conflicting views into the light that we can recognize where they may be blocking us from an opportunity to grow and learn.

Can you think of times in your life when you've developed a justification and acted irrationally when confronted by something that doesn't match your world view? It can be difficult to avoid. Even as we recognize the strength in another person's arguments or see contradictions in our behavior, it can be hard to abandon the idea that we "know better." And even if we know something to be true, it doesn't always mean we will choose to act on it.

Nevertheless, by recognizing internal conflict, we gain knowledge about ourselves, our behaviors, and our world, and we open the door to being more open. We can't be open to that which we do not allow ourselves to see.

Recognizing cognitive dissonance is also key to critically thinking about the world around us. For example, advertisers capitalize on cognitive dissonance by creating contrary versions of reality for us to consume. Remember the Marlboro Man? He was created to give a rugged image to filtered cigarettes, which were considered feminine at the time.

Today, as we are inundated with studies on how terrible fast food is for us, fast food companies create advertisements featuring healthy-looking people doing activities, because they know our brains want to create consonance (i.e., agreement). The advertisers hope to match our understanding of what happens when we eat fast food with the image their ads present.

Be critical of what you hear and see! It is important to discern what is "really" being said. We are empowered when we can recognize these attempts for what they are and make our own decisions without being influenced by them.

One of the reasons we have such difficulty accepting views and ideas contrary to our own is that we look for examples that back up and support what we already think to be true. This tendency to believe something if it already aligns with our existing beliefs and ideas is called "confirmation bias."

As with cognitive dissonance, confirmation bias is an enemy to openness. It convinces us to see things in the way we already see them, rather than opening ourselves up to seeing them as they actually are. Confirmation bias is dangerous because it self-perpetuates. People actively gather, select, and interpret information according to their biases; even if the evidence is ambiguous, they will interpret information in such a way that it supports their existing position. It's easier to hear what we want to hear and see what we want to see, but it limits our point of view and potential growth. Biases are rooted in societal norms, which are always shifting. By adhering to biases, we put ourselves behind the curve of growth and miss out on a world of opportunity.

The term "confirmation bias" was first coined in 1960 by the English psychologist Peter Wason after conducting a test in which he challenged students to create a hypothesis about a rule involving a set of three numbers. He found that most people struggled to figure out the rule because they stuck strictly to their original hypothesis and didn't change it even when it appeared incorrect. Furthermore, they only tested their original hypothesis and did not form any others.

This simple experiment proved that people develop biases very quickly and maintain them. Once established, they do not easily open up to challenging their beliefs. Of course, in the case of this experiment, it was a belief they had just constructed; the effect of bias is much stronger for emotionally charged issues and for deeply entrenched beliefs.

When people hold strong biases, it results in a polarization of interpretations for the same information. Disagreement escalates even though different parties have access to the same "facts" and evidence. What makes this dangerous is that people who are uninformed or hold sympathetic beliefs, or who are part of the same social status, can be easily influenced to adopt these biases. Judgments are so often made on first impressions; even when subsequent information decisively proves an alternative interpretation is correct, many struggle to give this new interpretation the same consideration.

This is one reason the elevator pitch—where you sell an idea or yourself in the time it takes to conduct a short elevator ride (20–30 seconds)—is so important, and why it is also so difficult. A lasting impression can be made in those few brief seconds that may never be able to be changed or undone.

Another example of confirmation bias is when people falsely perceive an association between two unrelated events or people. The fact that you might be right about this association does not justify the means by which you arrived at this conclusion. True confirmation is based on evidence, not assumptions borne of bias.

The effects of confirmation bias are manifold—and can be seen at all levels of society, from our everyday lives to the world stage. When the United States went to war with Iraq, we were told by the American government that Iraq was developing weapons of mass destruction. Despite no evidence suggesting this was true, people were ready to believe it, which created the agreement to sanctions and popular support for the war.

Note that I am not suggesting that there were no good reasons to remove Saddam Hussein from power, but this example shows how irrational and emotional decisions can be made when the information provided preys on our tendency towards confirmation bias.

Biases are like blinders; they narrow our gaze to what we already know and believe. In this way, they are the anathema to what it means to be open. When we are open, we allow new truths to enter.

Have you ever been approached by someone whose life choices were different than yours? What were your immediate assumptions? Did you associate their abilities, ethics, and intelligence with how they were dressed, their ethnicity, their sexual orientation? It's hard not to jump to conclusions based on what we think to be true, but achieving greatness requires discipline to move beyond that first impression and judge people based on their merits and actions.

We grow up absorbing subtle and not-so-subtle prejudices from our parents, teachers, authority figures, siblings, friends, and mentors. The society we live in, the media we are exposed to, the culture we are born into, all imprint myriad beliefs and accepted truths within us that affect the way we see the world. These combined inputs establish our truth and value systems. Biases are neither inherently good nor inherently bad. Danger exists, however, when we don't recognize biases for what they are: deeply ingrained ideas about the world that affect how we understand it and act within it.

I am not telling you to let go of what you believe in, nor to embrace values you may not be comfortable with or those that do not fit into your value system. What I am saying here is that there is power in learning to listen, absorb, and consider other points of view, especially those from outside of our standard truth and value system. As a first step, we must accept that we all possess biases. That's natural and human. When we see our biases as inherent and as self-evident truths, and then use them to discriminate against those who choose to live differently, however, we don't just hurt and limit others; we hurt and limit ourselves. To bring about personal greatness, we must strive to be objective and open to all ideas without judgment. Letting go of bias is fundamental to being open and making decisions that will lead us onto the path of greatness.

When I first read Leonard Mlodinow's *The Drunkard's Walk* (2008), I found that it activated in me a knee-jerk defensiveness and disbelief, which is precisely the barrier to openness that we are discussing. In his work of alternative thought, Mlodinow writes about the concept of "heuristics" (approaches to solving problems that work as a guide—a rule of thumb—if you will) as an introduction to his assertion that people mistakenly believe they can predict and manage the randomness they see in their lives. Hence, the title of his book. In fact, Mlodinow argues that people are inherently poor at perceiving probabilities (somewhat understandably, as probabilities are based on events or circumstances occurring hundreds, or millions, of times— something humans rarely observe), so they rely on biases to make decisions. This realization is a vital insight that confirms the massive influence our biases have on the decisions we make even when, possibly especially when, we believe we are being rational and thoughtful. When we are unaware of our biases, we close off many avenues for opportunity.

Mlodinow goes on to argue that, because we are unable to perceive probabilities in a meaningful way, humans tend to minimize the effect of chance and randomness on events. Our fear and frustration about this randomness leads to a defensiveness that ensures that we hold on to our illusion of control against all evidence.

This is where Mlodinow and I part ways, however. While I concur with Mlodinow that chance does play a role in our lives, I would argue that a person's energy has a significant influence on events. We can, with a complete understanding of the role chance plays in our lives, attain a state where our decision-making processes are not driven solely by our biases but through the development and maintenance of a healthy intuition. Indeed, this state of being is core to our being objective. This is the place where the randomness in life works with us to propel us towards the life of purpose and success we seek. Our energy drives the outcome of randomness in our lives; it acts like a beacon of light illuminating the way for the universe to deliver.

Take the day I started the Links company. I was already operating a small warehouse, but that morning Limore and I toured a much larger facility. It was exactly what we needed in order to expand our operations, but with no clients lined up, it was more than we could afford. Regardless, we told the real estate agent to hold onto it and we would get back to her later that afternoon. Our next stop was a meeting with a team bringing Dave & Busters to Canada; I was pitching them a ROOTS-branded D&B clothing program. During our conversation, the team confided in us that they had run into a major problem with their operations. Containers of equipment were arriving, and they needed a space where their engineers could install card-swipe access technology for the gaming machines. Limore and I looked at each other. I told them we had just such a place. They gave us a one-year commitment and the fees we charged covered the full cost of our lease, leaving us with plenty of extra space to rent out to other companies and turn a profit. By the end of that one day, we had new clients and a new warehouse—and we sold them the clothing program to boot.

This is just one example of a moment I've experienced when I had a need, and by being open and positive, I was able to see the connection and potential opportunity that would fulfill it. It may sound random, coincidental, or even "lucky"—after all, we had walked into that pitch meeting with an entirely different focus and objective—but I've come to believe that there is nothing "lucky" about being able to see the connections of random events and making them work in your favor.

In fact, I would go even further and say that when you are open and infused with good energy, events don't look so random at all. I learned early on that there are no coincidences; if you make yourself available to serendipity and the unexpected, anything can happen. What looks random is in fact a reflection of the relationship between you and the universe. We can all be that unicyclist—achieving total balance with all the plates spinning.

Every time I walk out that front door, anything can happen.

Openness—and the creative process it births—originates in the mind-body-spirit connection. As an entrepreneur, it is crucial to understand the connection between the way I think, the way I feel physically and spiritually, and my performance in the field. I believe that everyone can benefit from recognizing these connections and then exploiting their potential. Many of us lead busy lives and typically have multiple demands that require our immediate attention. The pressure to perform and achieve can be intense. When you are in a position of leadership, the more people that are affected by your decisions, the greater this pressure can be.

In these circumstances, the mind-body-spirit connection is of critical importance. When you are centered and all these elements are healthy and in tune, you can remain energized and purposeful, yet be calm, open, and objective. In these moments, your intuition is at its most healthy, guiding you towards your personal greatness.

When I reach this place of healthy intuitive power, my "intuition" is almost autonomous; I can make choices faster than my mind can process all the inputs. This intuition is not an irrational actor. It is built on my openness, my expertise, and my experience.

Society trains us to trust our minds first and foremost, but your mind is often driven by motivations that are not necessarily congruent with healthy intuitive processes. The reality is that you do not always have the luxury of time to construct a detailed plan before making an important decision. Decisions often need to be made on the spot. It is only when the spirit and the mind align that you become your most powerful self. When this happens, anything is possible. Greatness is within reach.

> *I have come to a place of awareness and consciousness where everything around me produces and provides. I open myself to this world, beyond my biases. I am willing to listen, absorb, accept, and act. I experience the force of a trajectory that pushes me upwards and towards the finish line. All around me I see ideas and solutions.*

But one final ingredient remains. Even if you recognize the ways in which your pain gives you pleasure, even if you remove your biases, even if you embrace the mind-body-spirit connection, you cannot achieve greatness unless you "will" it to happen. This is a key that must be turned before you can unlock the power of tuning in.

Lidia, my late mother-in-law, worked with me for nearly fifteen years. She used to encourage me when I was feeling down by saying, "You are a cat that lands on all fours." That may seem true, but unlike a cat, my ability to right myself is not necessarily natural. My ability to land on all fours is the result of my fierce determination. I am often faced with what I would describe as "Field of Dreams" moments. In the movie with that title, Kevin Costner undergoes immense struggles as he builds a baseball diamond in the middle of nowhere, operating on faith in the form of a disembodied voice that repeats the phrase: "If you build it, they will come." I've thought about this voice many times over the years. Having a vision requires ignoring those people who set out to discourage or demotivate you, while placing faith in the future. Any success I have achieved has been foremost to do with believing in myself and staying the course.

I sometimes visualize myself as a hunter in another time. I am standing in the grassland, dressed only in some animal skin loin cloth. It's just me and my spear moving stealthily through the tall grassland. I must find my prey. Either I make the kill or I will go hungry. The sharper my spear, the straighter my arrow, the more agile I am—all these variables contribute to my success. I may not be able to control the peripheral elements, but I can be prepared, energized, and focused. At the end of the day, it is my will to take that shot that makes all the difference.

One practice that will help you tune in is creating a mind map. This involves writing ideas about a particular goal on a clean piece of paper in order to start to understand and visualize what you need to happen to achieve that goal. If you have never made a mind map before, try it. Think about a goal and then write it down in the center of a page, along with whatever random words come to mind that relate to that goal. Now take a step back and look at your creation; allow your intuition to make connections.

Without too much overt thinking, start circling words of interest and draw lines between ideas. When you are done, you will have a road map of tasks that will take you to the finish line.

I use this technique when coming up with a mission statement for a project, or when I require a series of steps to achieve an idea or to confront a challenge. It's kind of like the board game *Snakes and Ladders*. All the tasks form a winding path to your goal. Each roll is an opportunity to move you closer to the final square. The path is not, however, always linear. There are ladders that, if climbed, allow you to bypass long stretches to accelerate your progress. At the same time, there are snakes that will send you tumbling backwards farther away from your ultimate goal. As the old Yiddish proverb states, "Man plans and God laughs."

Being flexible is key to achieving your goals. Embracing flexibility is one of the most exciting and joyful parts of living a more open life. You roll that dice and start moving, never knowing exactly where your next step will take you. It is important, however, to not veer so far off the path that you lose sight of your goal.

Flexibility marks the intersection between openness and willingness. On one hand, you need to remain open to the dynamic flow of the universe bringing you solutions and ideas at every turn; on the other hand, your drive must keep you focused and disciplined in order to bring your goals to the finish line. The result of achieving the right balance can be magical. The slightest mishap, unplanned event, or rogue idea could actually be the best and biggest thing to happen to you. You sometimes have to throw the map out the window and just travel the road as it presents itself. Momentum is everything; you simply need to get started.

In 1996, I was invited to speak at a conference in Australia. The flight had a stopover in Hong Kong. A couple of days before I was scheduled to leave, acting on a fleeting thought, I asked my assistant to look into our leads database to see if anyone from China had inquired about Cybermind, the virtual reality technology company I founded in 1993. "No rock left unturned," is one of my mottos. Two names surfaced, and one answered our email. Emily was the heiress of a prominent family real estate company in Hong Kong and China; she and her driver met me at the airport during my 12-hour stopover, took me for lunch, and showed me some of the sights. Emily talked about her family's interest in expanding outside of traditional real estate and went on to explain her vision of incorporating an entertainment concept into one of their projects in China. We clicked; she was really in tune with what Cybermind was doing at the time. This random meeting resulted in a consulting relationship where I was directly involved in the design and build out of two sizeable projects in China, which marked a significant sale for Cybermind. A few years later, when I developed the brand Tek2go, I would go on to leverage my experiences in China as a gateway into the consumer electronics business.

When thoughts occur randomly in your head, your intuitive powers are telling you something. These thoughts are not random. Listen and trust yourself; be open to the possibilities; don't double guess yourself or give in to doubt. Trust that you are part of a greater plan and think of these thoughts as messages from a higher power. You always have a choice—to pass or to act. Take it from me, life is far more exciting and potentially lucrative if you trust yourself and choose to act.

During a Passover dinner in 2004, the conversation over dinner turned to product sourcing in China. Spontaneously, my friend Ernie, whose family were our guests, suggested he and I attend the Canton Fair in just a few weeks' time. I booked tickets the next day. The trip was memorable—I am often amazed by what a difference teaming up with the right person can do for your energy and perspective. Spending time with someone with complementary energy can go a long way to being in a place of openness. We walked through the miles and miles of show floor space at the fair when I came across a company selling a glass body-fat scale. I stopped in and *kibitzed* with the proprietor. I spoke Jewish; he spoke Chinese—we understood each other perfectly! I remember thinking in an instant, "Wow, that is great value for ten bucks!" That could have been the end of it. But my mind was open and I allowed my intuition to take charge. I knew the product had great consumer value. In fact, I was certain it could be branded and sold for $49.99. I saw the opportunity and I ran with it. I created a brand called Healthy Balance, designed the packaging, branded the scale, and sold thousands to mass retailers. I netted out $15 per scale. What had started out as a random conversation ended up becoming a cash cow. I had no experience selling body-fat weight scales; I did not do a business plan or market studies. I simply acted on my hunch.

Here is the thing: I was open to an idea, I was willing, I listened and trusted my intuition, and—here is the most important part—I took action. When I made that decision, I didn't have any guarantees as to the outcome—I hadn't made any sales or conducted any market research—but I believed in myself and I trusted the universe to deliver. I wrote the check.

This was not a unique or even a one-time event in my life. Over the years, I've become practiced at allowing myself to believe and thus have the confidence to take risks. There is always a tipping point between intention and action. In that moment, everything can happen or nothing can happen. To get to that moment, however, you need to be open to the possibilities and trust your intuition. Once you're there, you then have to find the hunger within you and let it out.

Do you know the old joke? A guy continually complains to God that he never wins the lotto. He keeps complaining until finally a voice booms down, "Buy a ticket!" It's not enough to dream or talk or wonder; achieving greatness requires taking action.

As success starts to become the norm for you, it is easy to become self-absorbed and self-serving; we may forget where we came from. Openness is about listening and continuing to learn. It's about projecting love to the world beyond yourself. Don't forget simple acts, like taking a moment to meet someone's eyes and smiling, making a positive comment about someone's appearance, or practicing acts of kindness. The positivity you put out into the world returns to you so many times over. One dreary afternoon I was jogging in Vancouver's Stanley Park, feeling rather low about a lumber mill deal that was not going my way. I was in the midst of taking over a company that had provided the trusses for the pre-fab homes I was building on the West Coast. A woman running towards me smiled at me as she approached and we passed each other on the sea wall. I instinctively smiled back— and wow! Her smile penetrated deep inside of me. Suddenly I felt happy and grateful. The gray day changed and the sun came out.

I now do my best to smile at people I pass; you would be surprised at the difference it makes. It's a small act, but it can be a powerful booster whose positive energy reflects back on us.[3]

A big part of opening yourself up is to allow your own beliefs and actions to be challenged. A critique from a place of good intent can come from someone close or a total stranger; it can make a huge difference. Tuning in is about learning to listen, especially when confronted with ideas that generate an emotional, defensive reaction. When I presented the manuscript of this book to my friend Randall Craig, after three years in the making, I was pretty sure it was done. He was pretty candid in his review and about what I needed to do next. Listening to him and taking it back for a rework made this final product so much better!

If we listen to criticism without defensive posturing, the benefits to our projects, ideas, and lifestyle can be powerful, driving us further towards personal greatness. The best critique is not an admonishment or judgment, but rather an objective insight from someone who cares. Mentors in life can be rare; when you come across a person willing to provide thoughtful

---

[3] As it turned out, the lumber mill deal would not have been a good idea, and what I could not see at the time was that the deal falling through was a blessing in disguise. Sometimes, the best deals are the ones you do not do.

and insightful criticism, consider it a gift that you unwrap with intent and openness.

Openness requires vigilance. As you continue on this journey to achieving your greatest self, you will encounter times when life starts to spiral out of control, until you are eventually brought to a reactive space where you depreciate. We are all subject to human failings. You can't stop every bad thing from happening, you can't anticipate every setback, and you can't wake up every day feeling invincible. We all have demons inside us that find pleasure in our pain. These instances are not a sign of failure; they are an indication of our humanity.

When you recognize these setbacks, or recognize that you are on a negative trajectory, you have the opportunity to make changes and alter your momentum. When I find myself in a reactive mode, the best solution for me is to come to a dead stop. I remove myself from the situation as quickly as I possibly can. Think of it as an emergency brake. If you hesitate to pull it, you could cause potentially irreparable damage. I might leave the office and go for a run, read a book, clean my house, or cook an elaborate feast. Sometimes, it is only with this distance that you can open yourself up to recognize, in the classic Bergler-esque sense, that *I am in a reactive state because I put myself here.*

The best thing about being open is that by recognizing this state, you come to know yourself even better, thus setting yourself up for future success.

Once you embrace openness, you are tuned in and are now in the game. Anything can happen. In this brave new world, there are no signposts to follow and no guarantees. That's the start of the fun! Trusting your intuition and taking action is what the pursuit of greatness is all about. We all battle self-doubts and fear failure. There are a great number of unknowns that exist between that "eureka" moment when an idea is born and the endgame when it comes to fruition.

It is impossible to plan for all contingencies, or to anticipate the path that will lead to success. Over-analyzing alone has led many smart and talented people with great ideas to abandon any hope of reaching the finish line before they even get started. Pursuing greatness is a risk, but there is a game-changing secret: You have something in your arsenal that defies logic but could make all the difference between success and failure. *Faith.*

Chapter Three

FAITH

The Art of Believing in a Greater Power

Without faith a man can do nothing; with it all things are possible.

-Sir William Osler

Faith is a belief that with each step you take you will find solid ground. In this chapter, I will prove to you that there exists a power that works in concert with all that sustains humanity. When you recognize it, you can give up the illusion of control and come to believe in something much larger than yourself that will deliver good things to you in the right time.

In modern Western society, we have a complicated relationship with faith. Overloaded with information and constant communication, we find ourselves in a sort of permanent rush hour, speeding from one task to the next, endlessly engaged. It is easy to get caught up in consumerist cycles of needing and wanting. When we stop to reflect and recognize the overarching narratives that guide our lives and our society, faith isn't often one of them, despite the fact that even if we do not realize it, we often operate on faith, rather than fact. For example, we believe it is rational to invest in buying a house because its market value will steadily increase and we will not only have a place to live but we will make money. What we have trouble recognizing is that this is not a fact but a belief. The belief speaks to an unquestioning faith in the free market system, believed to be in perpetual growth, along with the sanctity of real estate ownership. These beliefs are only revealed as "faith" in the system as opposed to "facts" of the system when challenged by certain events.

After the market crash of 2008, whole neighborhoods in the United States were abandoned when home values dropped below what was left owing on them. In this case, perpetual growth and free market systems were shown to be fallible. Investments that people thought of as rational and "can't-lose" turned out to be the result of misguided faith in a corrupt system. It wasn't until the bottom fell out that the pyramid scheme was revealed for what it was.

In the case of the housing market crisis, our faith was misplaced, but the reality is that all the societal systems we depend on are undergirded by faith. Even the use of paper currency requires a belief that it can be exchanged for something material; we give it value through our collective belief in its value. Note that I am not saying that all faith in these systems is misdirected, but I believe we risk taking our lives—and the world we live in—for granted if we don't recognize where faith operates and then work to balance our faith in systems with our faith in ourselves to recognize the truth.

I admire the contrarian, who has so much faith in themselves that they are able to go against the current of public belief. Don't doubt what you see right before your eyes. If the king is not wearing any clothes, he's not wearing any clothes. If it doesn't make sense, then it doesn't make sense. Sometimes faith in ourselves is the only thing keeping out the noise and distractions so we can make decisions with clarity and confidence. It takes courage and strength to go against the popular thought of the day—I have experienced situations where people simply do not want to recognize that something does not make sense. Look for yourself, the king is not wearing any clothes!

In his book *Malaise of Modernity* (1991), Charles Taylor critiques a self-serving rationale that emerged in twentieth-century capitalism he called "instrumental reasoning." This is the idea that we should use the "most economical application of means to a given end." In other words, all can be justified in the name of capitalistic efficiency. The fallout of this is that it contributes to a sort of solipsism in people and companies; instead of seeing the bigger picture, they focus on "number one."

Many of us have a drive for material goods and comforts, as well as a competitive pull for the prizes of success. But when we become too fixated on these motivations and employ instrumental reasoning to achieve them, we risk becoming disconnected from people, places, and situations around us and close off our view of the bigger picture. When we use instrumental reasoning, we are engaged in short-term thinking. We are thinking of the next prize, rather than the larger journey to sustained success and personal greatness.

These require a different sort of thinking, which Taylor called "collective reasoning." When we use collective reasoning, we see ourselves in relation to the world, as opposed to the world in relation to ourselves. This openness allows us to recognize patterns and connections all around us, and enables us not to get caught up in the reactive cycles caused by having a far narrower definition of ourselves. Expanding our horizons into the collective realm ensures that we remain grounded and "open" to seeing those things that seem to defy rational thought. When we do this, we start to see faith as faith itself and recognize the role it plays in our lives. It is only when this happens that we start to access the power of faith.

When we have faith, we trust that we will get to where we need to be in order to achieve our goals. We let go of our illusions of control and accept that the universe works in ways that, at times, may defy rational thought, but are in our best interests. We engage with the world on its terms, rather than trying to make it conform to ours. And then we let this powerful force push us towards our destiny.

I have plenty of reasons to believe in the power of faith.

The night I met my wife, the evening started out with my neighbor sweet-talking me into giving him a lift to this girl's birthday party. When I arrived, the hostess opened the door, wearing a black shirt with gold medallions attached—this first sight of her is engraved on my brain. She looked at me and the craziest thought immediately entered my head: *This girl will make a great mother to my kids.* I had never met her. I was seriously almost embarrassed; what was worse is that I felt like she could read my thoughts. Our eyes met for a split second—an eternity—and then she took my hand and led me to a table laden with food. It was a prophetic moment—more than 27 years and four kids later, she continues to sustain me. The night before we met I had convinced myself that I would never meet anyone and I would grow old alone; I gave up the illusion of control, then fate intervened.

Here's another story.

It was 1994, and I was working feverishly to launch my first start-up, Cybermind. I had invested everything I had, which was not much at the time, and had already committed to the equipment I needed, but after months of running into roadblocks, I still didn't have capital or a location. It was starting to look like the company might never get off the ground. That's when I landed a meeting with Ed Mirvish, a Toronto original, one of the city's most colorful businessmen and philanthropists (and founder of Honest Ed's, a discount store that was a city icon for over fifty years). I thought: *Finally, here's my break.* My plan was to rent out a space below the Princess of Wales Theatre on King Street. I showed up to the meeting and made my pitch. Ed must have been at least 90, and during my presentation, his sidekick, of the same vintage, kept falling asleep and Ed would nudge him awake with his elbow; it was a slapstick routine. Then, all of a sudden, Ed got serious with me. "Virtual reality?" he said. "When I close my eyes and go to sleep, that's virtual reality."

Not only did he think the idea was without merit, he would not rent me the location. Acknowledging my apparent disappointment, he went on, "You think that because you're a nice Jewish boy I'm going to give you a break?" he said. "This is business, sonny. I don't think it will work, at least not in this location, and I would not be doing you any favors." Ouch! That hurt. I will never forget the clarity and sharpness of his words.

Even at his advanced age you could see that below his gentle, humorous old-man demeanor, there was a shrewd businessman at work. I stumbled out the door into a drizzling cold February afternoon feeling like the biggest loser in the world. That's where this story could have ended, but it didn't.

Caught up in an internal dialogue of self-loathing and regret, I started walking without a destination. I shivered in the absence of a proper coat to protect me as the icy rain picked up. All that ran through my head was how stupid I had been, how badly disillusioned I was, thinking that I could make this idea happen. For the first time in this odyssey I lost total belief in what had brought me there. I hit rock bottom. My legs moved without any real direction, and when next I looked up, I was standing beside the CN Tower. I put my hand out to touch the cold concrete and as I stood there, it struck me that this icon of the city, once the tallest building in the world, started out as an idea in somebody's head. Yet, here it was, the coldness of the structure beneath my hand, a tower jutting into the sky.

Awash with self-pity, and by this time, drenched and cold, I walked into the building in a sort of daze, and I remember wondering: *How did this structure come to be?* I sat down in a lounge area on the ground floor near the elevators. Children gripped their mothers' hands tighter as they walked by; I must have been a keen sight. As I sat there, I couldn't help but notice that the elevator doors kept opening and every time they did, at least 30 people walked out and passed me as they left the building. I wiped my eyes with my sleeve and pushed back my hair, and for the next two hours, I counted the number of people who walked out of that elevator. It wasn't long before different emotions started to emerge: hope and excitement.

The vision came to me. The passion returned. I had my answers; I knew exactly how I would do it. I knew why it would work. It made sense. I walked into the administrative offices of the CN Tower and told the receptionist I wanted to speak to whoever was in charge. "Do you have an appointment?" she asked. "No," I had to admit. Hell, I hadn't even had an idea I wanted to speak to someone until just then. She told me I had to call in and send a proposal. That did not work for me. I had already seen a name on one of the doors and I walked past her and into an office.

I could hear the nice lady call security and I knew I had about 10 seconds to make my case. The guy behind his desk looked up at me skeptically. I told him I was here to rent some space. "We have none available," he countered. I tried again, "I'm going to pay you $300 per square foot for it." At that moment, his receptionist came barreling through the door, but he raised a hand and she came to a halt. "And how are you going to do that?" he asked, and I was in.

Twenty-four hours later, I had a lease for 1200 square feet of space in the CN Tower, right in the very space I was feeling sorry for myself. Cybermind's flagship store location was born. It was a great deal for the CN Tower, which stood to make good money off dead space, and it was a great opportunity for Cybermind. Three months later, we launched. Police had to be called in to control the excitement of five-dollar wielding adventure seekers who wanted to be among the first to fight pterodactyls among other network players in virtual reality. Determined to open as planned, I was up for nearly 72 hours readying the space for our launch.

As the lines started to form, I remember collapsing on one of our black leather couches and feeling this enormous sense of accomplishment. People were trying to speak to me, but for a moment, everything went quiet. My emotions were deep; I remember laughing, crying, but more than anything else I recall looking at the sun's light pouring through the window and seeing myself as that seven-year-old who stood in the tall grass of the backyard and imagined that one day his life would be amazing. I reveled in a powerful reverberation of the faith and destiny I felt that day. Here, in a moment of incredible personal success, as I stared at that same sun, everything I had been through came back to me, and I realized that I had started to deliver on the promise I made to myself that long-ago day. That night I slept more deeply than I had in years.

As it turns out, Ed Mirvish was absolutely right. What he said that day was hard to swallow, but he knew his business, and he knew that his theatre was the wrong location. If he had been a nice guy and rented it to me, Cybermind would most certainly have failed. Location was everything. People weren't going to seek out virtual reality as a regular Friday-night activity; it belonged in a destination location like the CN Tower, with an attentive transient audience of people who were in adventure mode. It was an impulse buy. Every single person who walked out of that elevator walked straight into Cybermind. That was the key to our success. It turned out that Ed rented the space below his theatre to Druxy's deli. *Dinner before or after a show? Now that makes some sense, too!*

───────

At times in my life when I have found myself struggling, something happens that is difficult to explain. By letting go of biases and being open to the power of faith, miracles start to happen and the answers I seek appear. In fact, it's happened so often that I've started to anticipate when to let go and let this mysterious force do its work. For many people, this can be hard to accept, especially for those of us who are invested in the idea of being in control. The belief in this force of faith does not mean surrendering any power; in fact, the opposite is true. When you allow yourself to have complete faith and recognize the power of the universe, you will discover that unpredictable things happen, feeling as if they were meant to have happened. In fact, the less you try to control your life and the lives of others, the more in control they become. Sounds counterintuitive? Sure, but it's also true. That is why it is important to make a conscious effort to access faith. Trust that you can move through that wall. Give yourself over to faith in a universe that loves and provides.

So, what exactly is this mysterious force of faith? Each of us has to answer that question for ourselves. Chances are we will arrive at a slightly different version based on our backgrounds, our cultures, and our experiences. In this book, I want to share the journey I took to arrive at my own interpretation of faith, in the hopes that it will help you find your answer.

From an early age it was drilled into me that there was one God and that *He* was all-powerful and would control every outcome in my life. There was a simplicity to this construct. One word. One true faith. One way to see and interpret the world. People naturally gravitate towards this sort of structure because it removes all doubt. But I have witnessed firsthand how religious dogma can breed tyranny. Organized religion is man-made, not God-made. And often, what is created of the human hand is motivated by the human need to control.

Spiritual belief and religious adherence are not one and the same. The former can exist despite organized religion; the latter requires obedience to the strictures a society imposes. My upbringing was very restrictive, and my life lacked the joy of a healthy childhood. Religion was used as a tool of oppression and, at times, abuse. I witnessed people use their interpretations of God to subjugate others. It was violence done in God's name and I never could reconcile this with a creator who preached the sanctity of life above all else. I knew this was not God's intent, and yet by the time I left my home for good at 16, my relationship with God had been severely compromised. And then something changed.

When I started out on the journey described in this book, I realized I needed to free up space in my mind, heart, and soul where I was harboring pain and anger from the injustice of the world I grew up in. If I was going to move forward, I needed to forgive. Once I allowed myself to forgive, and I was no longer beholden to my past, I felt like I was finally free to develop my own set of beliefs. I realized that, to me, quite simply, "faith" is love, and "love" is the energy that fills our souls with life and creativity.

This love is nourishing and warm and all-encompassing; it is like a mother's womb, giving, protecting, and providing; filling us with the optimism to create, produce, and contribute to the circle of life. A circle that widens with every breath we take. For me, there is a religious element to this faith. At some point, I decided that I wasn't willing to surrender my relationship with Judaism due to the actions of others. I believe in the trueness and oneness of God and take comfort in the idea of a power much larger than myself. However, my Judaism is not about repression or forced compliance; it's a celebration of goodness, spirituality, and love rooted in a commitment to others.

This is my vision of the force that fuels me. But it needn't be yours. For some people, the idea of God may align with more traditional religious teachings. Others will associate this force with the natural world; still others will find it in the concept of fate or destiny. No matter the descriptive branding, what is common is the recognition that there are forces larger than the individual that are at work in our world; aligning with these forces will be a strong guiding force for you as you achieve personal greatness.

Giving up on the notion of control allows destiny to do its job, but it is not always easy to accept or believe in the power of faith. This point hit home as my daughter prepared to apply for law school. It was September and we were spending the weekend at Lake Rousseau, one of my happy places; the stillness of the water wrapping itself around the many little treed islands, the morning mist, and the smell of cedar. Even getting there makes me happy, as I wind through the townships and over the narrow bridges that separate the lakes connected by the Welland Canal system. I love the independent ice cream store with its worn wooden steps bowed in the middle from years of happy feet coming and going. Over dinner, my daughter, Arielle, opened up about some of her fears and anxieties—law school admissions, career path, relationships, money. I smiled; these are exactly the sort of things that she should be worrying about at this time in her life—they point to a desire to live in a productive and meaningful way—but for Arielle, all the not-knowing, the uncertainty, was hard to deal with. Arielle was articulating something that plagues many of us. "Your problem is that you want to control everything," I told her. "But how do I know I'm making the right decisions?" she protested. "How do I know that being a lawyer is the right choice? That I'll like law school when I'm there? How is it possible to know these things when you haven't yet done them?"

Arielle is of course correct. You can do all your research, go to school in preparation, and trust your intuition—and there is still a final leg of the journey that you cannot control. The fact that she was able to articulate that anxiety is huge, however. People really run into problems when they are anxious about something but cannot put it into words. Verbalizing the source of the anxiety is half the battle to countering that scary feeling and starting to deal with the unknown.

During the early 90s, when developing photos was actually a thing, I used to get my films developed at a shop across the street from the townhouse I lived in. The proprietor was an interesting chap, an Indian Jew who once served in the Israeli air force. "You have nothing to lose," he would say. "Don't squander your opportunities—now is the time to take risks." He was right, and his words became my motto—as a young man with no attachments, I had nothing to lose. Taking risks was the only way I could move my dreams to within reach.

The only way Arielle will know for sure what she wants, the only way she will figure out where the path will take her, is to walk it. *But does that lesson still apply in midlife, when many of us have a lot more to lose?* I would argue a resounding: *Yes!*

As an entrepreneur, my real vocation is managing risk; it's the only way for me to expand my business and I'm so used to taking risks that it's become second nature for me. That being said, I have to admit pulling the trigger, no matter what due diligence I've undertaken, is counter to my instinct to preserve personal capital. I recognize that for most people taking risks can be a very scary experience; I've seen people so upset at the proposition of risk it makes them physically ill.

The reality is that there is risk in everything we do. Even if you think you are not taking risks, you are. It can be risky to stay at the same job for years; it can lock you into one industry, or one career path, or one set of skills, even if it feels riskier to set out and try something new. I was pretty nervous walking down the aisle. Guests joked that I was whiter than the bride's dress. It wasn't that I was unsure about what I was doing, I actually took it all very seriously, but I was terrified remembering my parent's unhappy coupling—I really wanted this to work! When I gave up control, the universe delivered ten-fold.

In those moments when you place your trust in the power of the universe and believe in your future, you jump off that ledge into the unknown—it's a thrilling moment. The more you believe in yourself and the healthier your intuitive powers, the more comfortable you will be with letting go of control and putting your faith in the universe.

As we watched dusk descend over that crystalline lake, this is what I told my daughter. "Make peace with the control beast," I said. She laughed. "But really," I said, "we're here now. Let's make the journey fun." I don't know where Arielle's path will ultimately lead her, but I trust she will find her place and her purpose.

Understanding that there is a powerful guiding force out there, one that is larger than you, is only the first step. Now, you need to understand how to tap into this force in order to realize your dreams. When I look back, I am grateful beyond words that the dreams I dreamed in the isolation of my childhood have come true, many times over. Knowing what I needed to happen in my future and having faith, I made the commitment to do everything within my power to make those dreams come true. It's when we stop dreaming and hoping that our faith in the possibility of good things happening diminishes, and from there, life becomes a slippery slope towards despair. It takes a willingness to believe in that which we cannot see or touch, that is beyond our reasoning. But when we do, we open ourselves up to the potential that anything and everything is possible.

Faith will allow events in your life to turn out as they are meant to. These things cannot be forced to happen the way you want, nor when you want. There is a time for everything. In his friendly South African drawl, my friend Daniel asked me, "Israel, are you in control of it all?" I have been challenged with this existential question many times. *Can I control the universe or does it control me? Does life happen to me? Or do I make life happen?* The reality is, I believe we can control the universe to the extent of committing ourselves to actions that give us the best chance for success. That said, where would I be today if I had resisted and tried to control it all? It's impossible to say, but when looking back at the trajectory of my life there are so many opportunities I would have missed. The first thing you need to do in order to tap into the power of the universe, is to let go of your need for control.

In the next chapter, I will speak at length on the power of visualization, but let's do a simple exercise now. Keeping your eyes open, imagine a beautiful white dove that represents all of the things in life you are steadily working on. Inside the dove, visualize all the things you are trying to control—deadlines, colleagues, supply logistics, time, money, etc. Now cup the dove firmly in your hands and raise it above your head. Take a deep breath into your abdomen and exhale. As you do so, open your hands and in slow motion watch the dove fly up and away.

Now do this again with your eyes closed. Move your arms apart as you let the dove go and raise your head to the sky to watch it flap its wings and fly off into the horizon.

In this visualization, the dove represents all that you wish to control, and your hands represent the containment of those things. The horizon the dove flies towards is your future. The wonderful large breath you breathe and exhale is your release. That release is you allowing yourself to wholly give yourself up to the universe and to allow the universe in to deliver. It's okay to feel like something has left you, because, in fact, it has. The strappings that bound you from within have been unshackled and you can finally breathe.

As you go through this exercise, I guarantee you will feel as if a weight has been lifted. This is the feeling of letting go and placing your belief in something larger than yourself. The physical manifestations of your stress—the pains and closed feelings in your gut—should vanish, along with the weight that has been keeping you down in that reactive space. You will soar and gravitate to your greatest self.

> *I am doing everything I can do. I can only do what I can do. And having done my best, I can accept the outcome.*

Say this mantra out loud. These words will remove the anxiety of the moment, which is a negative pull against your confidence. Listen to the words and affirm that there is a master plan, and that you are part of it.

~⁓⊃

We hear this phrase all the time: *Timing is everything.* So many of us are naturally impatient, and this impatience is only heightened when we near the finish line of a project. We just want to get there already! But rushing things can hurt our chances of success. Having faith that everything has its time can be a powerful opportunity to allow us to take advantage of the unexpected.

With any project, I try and take a step back to make sure I'm not forcing something to happen on my timeline, before it's ready. I am a firm believer that things happen when they're meant to. If we try to force something to happen (outside of its time), we often miss out on the unpredictability of the positive events that can occur when the universe is working with us. There is a crucial point when it becomes vital to cede control and just let go.

At this point, the more we try to control the endgame, the more actions become reactive and repel the destiny of things that are meant to happen in the right time. The result is that the thing we most want to happen starts to retreat, producing further anxiety and potentially sabotaging the creative process. It's hard work to put all the pieces in play in order to reach the point where you can take your hands off the steering wheel and give up control. At that moment, it's a matter of faith to believe that all things will come together and happen as they are meant to. Repeat this mantra.

> *I have done everything I can. There are forces beyond my control. I am so grateful to have come to this point. I embrace these challenges and I believe that I will come to a place where I am meant to be.*

I figure that if I'm doing what I am supposed to do to get to where I'm supposed to go, I will not fail. We all strive for success, but don't make the mistake of equating a lack of success with failure. When you do everything you can to succeed you will never fail. The success that is meant to occur will come from the positive momentum created by your commitment and effort. The danger is when we end up in reactive territory, fighting to stay on a path that is not meant for us, kind of like running up an escalator the wrong way. My experience has shown me the benefits of not trying to control everything, and at some point simply allowing the universe do its thing.

My experience in the start-up world is that when you first have an idea or start a project, you have a very optimistic outlook. You are naturally excited and you may start telling people and jotting down plans, but often what happens next is you start to question yourself. The details seem to lose focus and clarity starts to slip; your confidence gives way to self-doubt. Pretty soon, there's that voice. *But how?* it whines at you late at night. *It's too hard. It's too uncertain. It's not going to work out!*

That voice lives in the heads of people who walk around and say: *Would have. Should have. Could have.* Three phrases that lead down the path to regret. That's the voice of that guy who sees something on TV and says, "Hey, they stole my idea! I thought of that years ago!" When you forge your own path, voices reflecting societal and conventional norms can be discouraging. As open as you are to the possibilities around you, there will always be naysayers. They will pepper you with all sorts of questions, trying to make you doubt yourself. Don't let that negativity in. In fact, use their questions to develop your pitch.

Once you work through enough of these conversations you should be able to pitch a good idea, as you will have the answer to every question! Verbalization of your ideas is part of the creative process. Use everyone you come across as a guinea pig, but don't let them erode your self-confidence. The magic happens when what you have to say comes from a total belief in yourself.

If you are meant to be on the path that you are on, the universe will find a way, even when you can't. When you realize this fact, you will have stumbled upon one of the secret ingredients for success; if you focus on "what" you need to happen—you articulate your goal—the universe will supply the "how." That is the power of faith.

Being clear on your endgame goal is key. The trick is to get away from primarily focusing on how something is going to happen and instead funnel your energies into what needs to happen. If you obsess over the "how" part of the process, it will drain your energy and sabotage your ideas. If I expended my energies and time getting the answer to how I was going to do something before I proceeded, I would never get out of the starting gate. Remember, our greatest explorers could only map out their journeys once they had confidently voyaged into what was then the unknown. It is no surprise that many of them, like the fur trader David Thompson who mapped most of Canada, were extremely successful entrepreneurs. Thompson had no map, only the passion and guts to discover. Having faith in the universe can make all the difference between action and inaction, success and failure.

Let me give you another example. Jason and I are business partners in a real estate venture called Stay at Blue Mountain—but that is not how we started. We purchased a single property together. We figured we would fix it up and we could take turns using it with our families. Our goal was to rent it out and utilize it when it was not being rented. Pretty soon we were so booked we couldn't use it ourselves, so on the one weekend we managed to get up to the mountain with both our families, we took a walk around, saw another property, and bought it. We rationalized that if the business didn't work out, we'd have a vacation property for each of our families. Soon after, we bought another chalet, and then we were approached privately about another group of properties in the same cul-de-sac and we had to make a quick decision before they put the property on the market.

One problem: we didn't have pre-approved funding, something we would need to come up with by the closing date. The truth is, we did not even consider the challenge of financing. We simply acted without questioning how we would pull it off. We intuitively knew that the business was good and we were meant to do it together, so we took the leap, put down our non-refundable deposit, and got to work on the business plan. A few weeks before the closing, however, we started to get nervous. We still had no investors or funding. I looked at Jason and said, "I don't know how, but we will find the money."

The very next day he left to go up north and he took a right instead of a left on the exit to grab a coffee. The Tim Horton's was housed in a building with a bank adjacent, so on a hunch, he walked in and asked to speak with a commercial mortgage specialist. Two days later, the bank extended us a $1-million line of credit, and we closed on the property. That was a nail biter! Can you imagine if we focused on our anxiety? Instead, we believed in our passion and kept moving forward. Within five years, we acquired over $8 million in income-earning assets and we never got buried in "how" we were going to do it.

In October 1994, when I signed the CN Tower lease, I had no idea how I would come up with the capital to fund Cybermind. Once I had my location, however, I raised the money within a couple of weeks. People get so wrapped up figuring out what comes first that they forget about the vision and passion that started the journey to begin with. Here is a news flash. You will rarely ever line it all up in advance. What you need is the belief that when you are doing something you are meant to be doing, all the things that you need will come into play. I have launched multiple companies using this philosophy. Stay at Blue Mountain today hosts thousands of people a year in the town of Blue Mountains.

At its peak, Cybermind employed over 600 people. Another company I started, Links, fed me for nearly 15 years before I was bought out.

Here's a story. One Monday morning in 2006, I walked into the Links offices and the warehouse manager told me that our homegrown inventory management system had crashed and was unrecoverable. That software ran our business, so it was a huge problem. That afternoon, while we were still trying to come up with a solution, I attended a charity golf tournament (a rare event as I only ever play golf when it's a charity event—needless to say, I'm not a great golfer!). In the clubhouse, sitting on the auction table, was a packaged software box boasting inventory management capabilities. I did a double take as if I was on an episode of *Candid Camera*. I figured, *Why not?* and bought it for a $500 contribution. It turned out that the software was an extremely powerful database tool, which we were able to modify to suit our needs. What was a crisis for us in the morning was resolved by the afternoon. But that is not the end of the story. The name of that software was AdvancePro, and six years later I would become its CEO. Discovering that software box that day was not simply a coincidence. There is a highway of opportunities out there that you can jump on. Embrace an attitude of openness, and let faith in the universe be your "how."

Getting the universe to work for you isn't hard, but it takes some fine-tuning to know when to push and when to be patient. For my son Eitan's 19th birthday, I rented out a schooner complete with captain, and we sailed out of the Herzliya (Israel) port. It was a great time, especially when the toughest of his IDF army buddies started heaving over the side of the boat. The captain encouraged each of us to take the wheel, and when my turn came an analogous thought occurred. There is a certain faith to sailing, that with discipline, patience, and trust, the boat will respond to the course being set and the winds will fill the sails and propel you forward. When you have faith, it's a power unlike any other, and it can truly propel you to places you've never imagined, and to heights you could only dream of.

We all have days when our faith falters, but if we take action anyways, with the belief that it will return, we can stay the course. The unpredictability of the universe means that we may not understand how it will work looking forward, but when looking in the rear view mirror, we can see how it all fits and makes sense.

A belief in a power larger than any one person is a guiding source. Say this mantra out loud.

> *I am living in a universe I cannot control. At the same time, I can take action to provide the best opportunities for the outcomes I seek. I will trust it will all make sense in time.*

In the TV series *Star Trek: The Next Generation*, Captain Picard, played by Patrick Stewart, would consult with the character Guinan, the bar hostess on the Enterprise played by Whoopi Goldberg. She would just calmly answer Picard's questions, but she would not usually answer the question he asked, but the one he did not know how to ask. In our lives, we are the captains of our ships, going "where no one has gone before," and when we are faced with decisions to make or directions to follow, we too should consult the knowing oracle of our inner being for knowledge and guidance.

As you come to believe more and more in yourself and accept that you are loved and worthy, the answers will be there. You just need to ask the right questions and listen to the answers. Having faith can be summed up with these simple rules:

1. I am not in control.
2. I will do everything in my power to make my goals happen.
3. I will allow myself to believe that whatever needs to happen will happen—I only need to ask for it (and be grateful in return).

To move forward in your journey, you must first set your sights on the road ahead. This is your *future*.

Chapter Four

VISUALIZE YOUR FUTURE

You cannot connect the dots looking forward; you can only connect them looking backwards. So, you have to trust that the dots will somehow connect in your future. You have to trust in something — your gut, destiny, life, karma, whatever. This approach has never let me down, and it has made all the difference in my life.

-Steve Jobs

I can tell you one thing about the future with absolute certainty. It's coming, whether you're ready for it or not. There's no holding back tomorrow. We all know this to be true on some level, yet many of us live our lives in a way that suggests we don't "believe" it's true. The future can feel like a destination that never quite arrives. Like a carrot that dangles just out of reach. This makes it easy some days to slip into thinking about the future passively, or not at all. *One day*, we think, but that day forever lingers around the corner.

This apathy towards the future can create a situation where we stumble from one thing to the next, deferring dreams and goals instead of taking ownership of what's to come. This is a tragedy. Finding your greatness requires faith in a future where you will reach your destiny. If you don't have this mindset, what is there to look forward to? How can you strive to be your best? Just getting by, day in and day out, does not inspire creativity. Your belief in your future is absolutely essential to becoming your best self.

The future is not a singular, monolithic entity; every aspect of our lives has a future. Our career path, our health, the relationships that surround us. Together these futures create a spectrum that determines what we can achieve. The most limited resource we have is time. Using time constructively is therefore a great motivator. When we expend time where we do not have a future, the effect can be demoralizing and decelerate our forward momentum, perhaps more than anything else I can think of. The realization that you have wasted your time on something that has no future or with people with whom there is no future can create a huge sense of loss.

Remember the pleasure-pain pattern introduced in Chapter One? When we behave in ways that cause us pain—including engaging in activities or relationships that do not support our future—it infects the next moment and each moment after. Accepting that your actions are motivated by this connection between pleasure and pain and taking responsibility for them is foundational to reaching a future that will bring out the best of who you are. We all face difficult choices in life. Knowing who and what we want to be a part of in our future, clarifies these choices and helps us to achieve our goals and dreams.

We all reach crossroads at certain times in life. At these junctures, we have the power to choose to take ownership over our future. I reached my first crossroads as a child. I recognized that the dysfunction of my home held no future for me, and I made a promise to myself that as soon as I could I would change the course of my life. I started a journal in which I made lists of what my life would be like when I was older. I did not realize it then, but I was charting a course for the future I wanted.

Embracing our future ensures that we never have to live with regret. Regret is a demon; it will suck at your life force and make your story one of grievance instead of triumph. When we don't take responsibility for our future, we are opening the door to regret. Watch out for phrases like "should have, would have, could have"—if these words often show up in your conversations, they may indicate a lack of accountability for how you ended up where you are. Even if you desire to change your circumstances, limit your use of these harbingers of regret—they are excuses and they focus on what did not occur in your life, rather than what did. You can only access the power to change your future by understanding the intentions and actions that led you to where you are standing today. If you do not take responsibility for your past or your present, how can you take ownership of your future?

The reality is that every day holds an unknown number of possibilities incubating and getting ready to be born: new people you will meet, opportunities that will present themselves, amazing gifts that life has yet to deliver. Not every opportunity will fit into your plan for the future, but the path to greatness involves seeing these opportunities for what they are and identifying who or what merits your time, passion, and energy.

The question to ask yourself is: *Will the things I'm doing today propel me to a future where I am my greatest self? Looking back in the rear view mirror, will I have spent my time wisely?*

If the answer to either of these questions is either *no* or *I'm not sure*, then it is likely time to take action and make the necessary changes to create the future you envision. The goal here is not to control what happens in the future; we can't. The seeds of the future are planted in the present at infinitum. But we can follow Steve Jobs' lead and instead look back to all the events, both big and small, that have brought us to this moment today.

In retrospect, it becomes clear that we did indeed have a great deal of control over the events that happened to get us to this place. Project this newfound knowledge forward and it is clear that one day a year from now or ten years from now, you will look back at today and tomorrow, and understand the choices you made and how those choices fit the pieces of your life together.

Your attitude and behavior, what you choose to believe, and the actions you take today will shape your tomorrow. Don't wait until a moment of reflecting upon the past to employ openness and faith. Be mindful of today. Every moment is an opportunity to navigate your life course. It's time to turn off the auto pilot.

The practice of mindfulness is key to understanding how our behaviors and actions today shape our future. Mindfulness is the psychological process of bringing one's attention to the internal and external experiences occurring in the present moment. The concept was made popular in the 1990s by Dr. Jon Kabat-Zinn, Professor of Medicine Emeritus and creator of the Stress Reduction Clinic and the Center for Mindfulness in Medicine, Health Care, and Society at the University of Massachusetts Medical School. He coined the term "mindfulness" in an attempt to secularize meditation by removing any mention of or allusion to enlightenment, reincarnation, or religion. With this rebrand, he believed he could open up the practice to everyone.

Being mindful requires an honest approach to one's self and a "stop-and-smell-the-roses" approach to the world. The result of this awareness is not some Zen-like trance but a heightened and conscious acknowledgement of the present. When we are mindful, we attune ourselves to the world around us; this requires honesty, attention, and patience.

Try it right now. Simply be aware of your breath. Inhale deeply, and as you exhale, acknowledge that this breath is your life force. As you breathe in, be conscious of your energy. Take the moment and consider all that you are grateful for in your life. As you breathe out, feel yourself flushing out the negative thoughts. Sit or lie down and just be. Be aware of these precious few moments in the "now." How does that feel?

Mindful practices like these can be incorporated into everyday life. My digital watch has an app that sends messages to me periodically, telling me to stop what I'm doing and breathe for one minute. I love it. Being aware of your breath, this automated action that sustains life, powerfully brings you into the now.

Every day presents opportunities. The moment you wake up, you have an important choice to make: how you're going to see the world today. The lens you choose will reflect your level of optimism and determine the attitude you take in response to whatever comes your way. It is easy to be anxious when it comes to the unknown. Being aware of the present reminds you to take stock of where you are in the moment. You are not a passive passenger in your own future; rather, you alone are its architect. The choices you make and the actions you take will determine what happens next. It's that easy. Look forward with anticipation about what's to come; the future is upon you, and you have a big role in deciding what it will be.

⟞⟋⟍⟍⟍⟋⟞

How do we reset back to a positive attitude when negative events threaten to throw us into reactive tailspins? How do we maintain the belief in our positive future at all times?

My wife's grandfather, Eliasz, was a survivor of the Holocaust. Everything that mattered to him was taken: his home, his mother, his father, his sister, his brother. Yet, he lived a full life and is one of the only people I've ever met who died on their own terms. The Sunday before he passed we were sitting by the pool on a beautiful June day and for the first time I beat him in a game of chess. "Check *macht*," he said on my behalf. When I started to playfully argue that he threw the game, he took my hand and gave me this intense look. "This win is yours," he insisted. "You did it!" It was his last game.

The following Saturday, I was with him in one of those privately draped rooms in the hospital's emergency ward. He drew me close and said, "Tomorrow you will start to sit shiva." He told me that his only regret was leaving "them" behind. Of course I knew he was speaking of his family. In 1939 he had escaped the city of Lodz at his father's urging, leaving his sister (Esther Perl) and parents (Mendel and Miriam) behind. Just days later, the Polish contingent of the Reich forced their Jewish neighbors into the infamous Lodz ghetto.[4]

Despite this horrific chapter of his life, Eliasz not only survived but flourished. He made the choice to live, and at the end, he radiated serenity and peace. He found meaning in his life by being open and having faith in the gift of life. His greatest revenge was to survive and create new generations to succeed him.

There are powerful lessons to learn from those survivors of the Holocaust who rebuilt their lives from the ashes of that terrible time. People who suffered unspeakable loss yet were able to move on to create a future. Consider this question: *How will the decisions*

---

[4] We later pieced together that Rubinowicz family were likely murdered at Majdanek, a concentration camp located in the outskirts of Lublin. When Limore and I visited the site in 2016, there was still a sense of terror in the air. To this day, crushed bone fragments continue to surface from the heaps of earth, the past refusing to be buried.

you make today matter in the last day of your life? It may be odd to think about death in a discussion about the future, but the two are linked. There is a tendency to think of death, like the future, in the abstract, to overlook its reality and the fact that it will be the final consequence and culmination of all our actions and choices. We like to imagine that there will always be time to fix something or do something, but the busyness of life conspires against meditating on existential questions like what it all means. Considering this question reminds us that there are bigger stakes to our decisions, and helps us clarify our priorities. The reality is that all we can count on is today. If there is something to fix, change, or renew, do it now. Greatness comes from living each day as if it's your last.

It's a powerful lesson, and one that Eliasz imparted not just through his example. I remember one time my son Eitan, who was nine years old at the time, was standing at the head of our dining table with me, monkeying around as I was trying to recite the traditional Friday-night *kiddush* (prayer over wine). Our entire family was gathered. Without thinking, I pinched him and he smarted, more likely from embarrassment than pain. Later that evening, Eliasz came up and admonished me quietly. He told me straight out, "You have to make the decision now about what future relationship you want with your children." It was a stark warning that hit its mark.

I am so grateful that he made me aware. His words sunk in deep and I recognized that he spoke to my future and the opportunity I had to have an impact on the course of my relationship with my children. Years later, I feel so blessed for the respect and love we share in our family. I think back to that evening and I thank Eliasz for that lesson: *The decision is mine as to how I act and that will determine the future of my relationship with my kids.* Look for these lessons; when they come from a place of love and respect, they can have a lasting legacy.

Another of the things that always struck me about Eliasz was his sense of gratitude. He made it a practice to always be thankful and to never take the good in his life for granted. When you think of all the positive things in your life and give thanks for them, you kick open the door to let the light and air back in.

Being actively grateful requires a conscious awareness of all the things you have to be thankful for in your life. "Counting your blessings" is an excellent way to dispel negative momentum. The trick to this practice is to say your list out loud, and if you prefer you can also write it down. The action has a visceral effect and makes the intent real. Among the things I feel grateful for is living in a hands-free Bluetooth world where no one looks twice when I am giving an impassioned speech to myself in the car on the way to the office. My grandmother, who would talk to the walls to vent and work things out, was not so fortunate.

But "Bubby" was on to something. Saying the words out loud and drilling down to the details of why you feel grateful imbues the process with meaning. For example, I might start my prayer of gratefulness with something like this: "I am grateful for my wife"—now I go into details—"her name is Limore"—go further—"she stands by me and believes in me and is truly with me"—more—"I can trust her and feel truly loved by her"—now move to a current reason for your gratitude—"last week when I announced …., she was encouraging to me as she always is"— now, the closer—"I am so grateful that she is part of my life and for the beautiful life we have built together."

I will then do the same for my children, naming each of them and talking about what makes them unique and why I am so thankful they are in my life. Be specific—your future is in those details. Now you try it. *I am grateful for.... Because.... And specifically when....*

There are many things in our lives to be thankful for. I will do prayers of gratefulness for my health and the ability to do the activities I love, like going on long walks in the conservation areas surrounding where I live. I express gratefulness for my career, the people I work with, and the opportunities that arise every day. And yes, I even express my gratefulness for the challenges I face.

When a dark cloud approaches, I will go out of my way to counteract the slide into negativity by talking about it out loud in a positive way, and expressing how fortunate I am that I can learn from this challenging experience. I spend time detailing my accomplishments and reminding myself to celebrate them. I like to surround myself with mementos of past positive achievements. A powerful positive motivator is to actively remind yourself of your significant accomplishments. When in a sales rut, I will encourage our sales team to look up some of the deals they have closed. "You see," I will remind them, "you've done this before, and you can do it again." Soon enough, someone will be waving a signed proposal in the air. Studying a past positive achievement is a good jump start to making new positive stories.

The prayer of gratefulness is not a one-time occurrence. To access its power, you must make it part of your routine. It is one of the most powerful tools you can employ to shape your future, and it's easy to do. Take a moment right now to come up with a list of things you are grateful for—it could be the weather, the food you're eating, someone in your life, or the challenges you've faced and overcome. Now take one of those things and expand upon it. *What is it specifically you are grateful for? Why are you grateful for it? What effect has it had on your life?* Take the time and say thank you. Bring this gratefulness into the now.

> *The cloud lifts. I am optimistic. I am strong. I am looking forward to my future. Those things that were weighing me down are gone and I feel lighter. I walk into my day with a smile and a sense of adventure, open to the possibilities that anything can happen today. I have the faith and belief that I am loved and entitled to succeed, and that the universe will deliver. While I may not be able to control everything that happens, I can take responsibility for how I deal with it all. I am back on the path to greatness, looking towards my future.*

If taking ownership of your future requires living for today, the reverse is also true. Living for today requires you to have some idea of where you want to be in the future. *What do you want out of life? What fulfills you?* As children, we grow up constantly asking for what we want. As we get older two things happen. We lose sight of what we really need and we get caught up in societal narratives of what we're supposed to want. We work vaguely in the direction of achieving goals that are set for us, rather than ones we set ourselves.

The simple question of what we want from our lives can be elusive. Separating the non-essential wants—the objects of our desires—from the things we want that will fulfill us and propel us forward is crucial. A two-year-old may want ice cream and stamp their feet until they get it. A two-year-old also wants security and unconditional love. One of these falls into the category of desire; the other into the category of need.

Note that there is nothing wrong with wanting things. The problem occurs when we cannot distinguish between these two types of wants. One gives us short-term gratification, but the other imparts long-lasting feelings of purpose. For example, I really want a four-door Porsche Panamera, but I also want to be able to afford my kids' tuition. We need to recognize that the choices we make will be directly influenced by which of our desires we prioritize. This choice can be affected by our emotional and intuitive health and stability, but to achieve personal greatness, it is important to be able to prioritize that which moves us forward on the path to our future.

Psychologist Abraham Maslow developed a theory of human motivation in 1943 now called "Maslow's hierarchy of needs." He believed that our choices and behavior are governed by five stages of needs: physiological, safety, social, esteem, and self-actualization. A person must have their needs met at each stage before they can move on to the next. The most primary needs are psychological, safety, and social; these create feelings of being secure, being loved, and belonging. The next level is esteem, which manifests as confidence and self-respect.

All of these needs must be met to reach self-actualization, where a person has the opportunity to achieve their potential by knowing what they want and what their purpose is. The reality is, however, that very few of us are fortunate enough to have all these needs met all the time. Situations in life may conspire to endanger our safety, or impact our social or esteem needs. When this happens, we must recognize what has happened and find a way to address it before it drags us down into a reactive space. When we successfully adapt and overcome these deficiencies, we have the opportunity to reach the final stage: self-actualization.

There is a great deal of effort involved when one or more of your needs is not met in early development. You are left to figure it out for yourself, and the unfortunate truth is that not everyone does. But if you do not confront, recognize, and deal with needs that were not met in your developmental years, it can be much harder to move on and grow.

As a child, my developmental needs went largely unmet; I did not feel secure in my home; I was isolated and did not feel love. As a result, I had very low self-esteem. The path of least resistance was not an option for me, so I had to do a lot of work to find ways to meet my most basic needs. In some ways this upbringing was a blessing, as it forced me to grow. Today, as I observe my middle-aged contemporaries, I can clearly identify those whose environments, wealth, and status made it easier for them to follow the path of least resistance; they glossed over their developmental gaps with distractions such as self-medicating, material consumption, and narcissistic behavior.

Because they've never had to address these gaps in Maslow's hierarchy, they have never developed a core purpose, a fact that they try to cover up but which is easy to identify due to their lack of empathy for others. These people are not necessarily bad people, but they lack the grounding and purpose necessary to grow and enact change in their lives.

Growing up, I always equated intelligence, education, and good breeding with advantage. I had a friend who grew up in a privileged environment; he had charm, looks, wealth, and smarts, and yet, a direction and use for his talents eluded him. I can now see how privilege can insulate and work against some, limiting them from reaching their potential. I've learned that it doesn't matter what background you have, we all have needs that we must address in order to clear the path to our personal greatness.

Creating a vision for your future requires deep self-examination. The psychological effects of unmet needs can trigger unconscious defense mechanisms that prevent you from understanding what you want and who you want to be. We need to accept and identify where our developmental shortcomings are, overcome the emotional pain of having not been provided for in these instances, and seek to mend them. A therapist or coach might be able to help with this process.

Clarity is very important. When people cannot identify the reason behind their self-depreciating behavior, they can become frustrated and lose their sense of core purpose, and by extension, the opportunity to become their best selves. Sometimes, the more someone has to offer in terms of skill, creativity, and intelligence, the greater the gap between their potential and their reality. It doesn't matter who you are or where you come from. When you arrive at a healthy place of having dealt with gaps in your developmental process, you will be far better equipped to prioritize your real needs over your sometimes short-term and superficial wants. This is the gateway to becoming the best version of yourself.

By recognizing what's most important to us, we can make choices that serve our deeper sense of purpose and meaning. This is not wholly about making sacrifices. If I could afford the Porsche and pay tuition—great! However, no matter the breadth of your resources, there is always going to be something that you desire that comes at the cost of what you really need. When this happens, having a sense of your future can put these decisions into perspective. Greatness is not a thing you can buy; it's the contentedness of having fulfilled your needs, found your purpose, and realized the future you dreamed of.

The realization that your time is a scarce non-recoverable resource has implications for not just how you spend your time, but who you spend it with.

Surround yourself with people you have a future with. An alignment of common objectives is generally a good indication that there is a future to be had. I once had a conversation with a man who was dating a woman who didn't want kids and didn't believe in marriage. He then proceeded to tell me that he would like both of these in his future. Both were wonderful people, with valid reasons for feeling the way they did, but their life objectives conflicted.

Here is what I told him: "When you find yourself not on the same page as someone in a relationship, ask yourself: Are you spending time building a future or wasting it on a relationship with none?" The answer to this question is not always easy, particularly when it comes to affairs of the heart, but by considering it, we make ourselves accountable, which then gives us a perspective that may serve us better in the long term.

We all have people in our lives who are "stuck" and struggling, and not ready to take the same journey we are. I'm not saying we need to abandon these people or relationships; what I am saying is that you have a choice to make about whether or not these relationships are part of your future. If you are going to continue to be involved with someone who does not share the same vision of the future you do, be accountable for that choice.

The danger comes when we feel like we lack agency to determine what relationships we are involved in. If we too feel stuck, these relationships can have a truly depreciating effect on our being. We need support to move forward. The relationships that will serve us best in the long term are ones with people who are engaged with us and our life and who invite our engagement in return. When a relationship ends, it's often hard to come to terms with all the time and effort we have expended on that person. This feeling of loss can drag us down. However, it is important to accept what happened, and learn a lesson from it: *Be stingy with your time and who you spend it with.*

When I was a young first-time father, the thought of buying a house was so far removed from my reality it had barely occurred to me. I remember visiting a friend who lived in a townhouse in a North Toronto suburb, and I remarked to him that I couldn't imagine being able to scratch together enough dough to buy my own place. He turned to me and said emphatically with total conviction, his words strong and predictive: "Before you know it, you'll own a much bigger house than this." It was the way he spoke that stayed with me; despite all the noise and distractions in my life at the time, his encouragement made something that felt impossible become possible.

When I look back it was not until that conversation that the idea of owning a house turned into something real for me. When I started to believe it was possible, I realized that owning a home was actually about my need to grow my family, and that this was inherently connected to my future and core purpose. I believe that is the key—a want needs to become real in order to become a need. You must fully visualize your needs to make them real.

Six months later, we bought our first home. Much of what my friend predicted, came to be. That evening, someone believed in me and somehow, by hearing that, I believed in myself. Knowing people who can express their honest belief in you without condition is very powerful. Whenever you can, surround yourself with these relationships; they will help you fulfill your dreams and realize the future you visualize.

⌐⌐⌐

Here is a simple task. Write down a list of what you need to happen in your life. The incentive is simple: *If you write it down, it will happen.* I find it a bit of a mystery how few people will actually complete this task. You would think with all the complaining people do, and the dreaming of what they want, that they would give this task a shot. But for some inexplicable reason, with pen and paper in hand, so many people become stumped.

Charting your future has everything to do with having clarity about what you want out of life. If you do not have this clarity, it becomes a challenge to actively believe in your own future. *What good are needs if you cannot imagine a time and a space where they are met?* And if you can't articulate your needs, life becomes a reactive cycle of events that catapults you down the path of least resistance into a future that takes you further away from your purpose or what you really want. The end result is that you limit your potential.

Visualizing your future is a critical ingredient to living in the moment, articulating your needs, and reaching a place of greatness. When I say "visualize," I mean it literally. The idea is to see in your head a moving picture in high-definition. In this vision: *What would the life you want look like? What type of person do you want to become? Who are you? Where do you live? Who are you with?*

It's okay to dream. Dreams allow us to uncover our true needs. There are a number of ways to spur conscious dreaming. I find that when I go for a good run, the endorphins kick in and I reach a daydream state that I can use to visualize ideas of the future. I come up with some of my best ideas after exerting myself through exercise. A friend of mine prepares his sermons and articles during a spin class.

Meditation exercises are another excellent way to bring you to a dream-like state where visualizations, ideas, and answers arise. This state occurs in *Shavasana* stage of a yoga practice and in the final waking moments after a deep sleep. The author and pioneer of past-life regression therapy, Dr. Brian Weiss, refers to this state between consciousness and unconsciousness as a hypnagogic state and believes that this is when we are most creative and insightful because we allow thoughts and ideas to freely roam in and around our minds without much restriction.

You can also achieve this state of being through some simple exercises. Try just sitting back and breathing in and out. Focus your attention on your intake of breath and exhalation. As you think about your breathing you will relax, and soon ideas will enter your mind on their own. Don't control them; just let them be there. Take note. Usually these are random, fleeting thoughts, but they can also carry answers. The more relaxed you are, the more you will enter this conscious dream state of mind. This practice also has the benefit of bringing you powerfully into the present.

We have talked about the hierarchy of needs and how early development can affect our behavior and—by extension—the choices we make. It is now time to place those ideas into context and create a vision of your future and who is to be a part of it. Let's make a plan.

Since I can remember, in an attempt to take control of my life, I have made lists of what I wanted. The most important items I wrote down on a little piece of paper in the tiniest printing. I would keep this list in my wallet. When I transferred wallets, I would also transfer the list. As time went by, I would cross out the items I achieved. I would often take this list out and rewrite it, renewing my commitment to the future, and at the same time modifying it to meet my new reality.

Looking back, I feel very fortunate and grateful that all my core dreams—and then some—have come true. Is it magic? Not in the Harry Potter sense. You cannot wave a wand to make something happen. That said, there is a kind of magic here. By identifying my dreams and elaborating them in detail, I took the first step towards making them real.

In business, we make business plans to identify what we call the "pro-forma" of the future. These plans are solid predictions based on good market research. Why shouldn't this work for our life plans?

To get started, write an executive summary that details everything you want from life. Now break it down piece by piece and add details for what each item should look like. Have the faith to focus on the "what," not the "how." *What do you need to happen six months out, one year, five years, ten years, etc.?* Flesh it out: *If you want a car, what brand and options will it have? If you want to travel, where? How? When? For how long?*

This list will be an evolving document, and it's okay to adjust it as your world changes. How you visualize your future today may be different from how you visualize your future tomorrow. For me, getting married and starting a family created a huge shift in my priorities and changed the way I thought of the future, as it should have. The important thing is to get used to creating a vision of what you want the future to be. The items on your list are your plan. Now that you've articulated them, you can use the practices of openness and faith to help the universe deliver.

Create a weekly, monthly, quarterly, yearly, and—yes—a five-year plan. Add as many desires as you can think of. Now, consider which of these items are priorities that feed into your core purpose, and eliminate anything that does not belong. Note that I have said nothing about choosing the most practical items. What does not seem practical today may come within reach as you achieve the goals you have set. Create three columns. The first column is the "What" column; enter the list of desires you have already written. The second column is the "How" column; leave this blank. The third column is the "Goals" column; here you will enter an explanation of why you are doing this and what you hope to achieve.

As I mentioned earlier, do not focus on the "how." Once you have identified the contents of columns 1 and 3, the answers to column 2 will surface and you will know what to do. This is how faith operates. You identify what you want out of life and then set goals. You put these ideas out into the universe. With time, the answers, the relationships, and the opportunities magically present themselves. As you bring each item on your list to the finish line, the sense of positive achievement is a huge confidence builder.

> *I've completed that—I took it to the finish line. It's happened. I could do this again. I can have an idea and make it happen.*

In his book *Man's Search of Meaning* (1946), Frankl explains that a person loses their future when they lose their personal meaning in life. He came to understand that it was those who believed they had a future and could derive meaning from the present who were most likely to survive not just the atrocities of the Holocaust but the years that followed their liberation. It is well-documented that many survivors of the Holocaust succumbed to their despair after the war. The German Nazi machine demoralized its victims and robbed them of their souls, and many could not see the purpose of going on living.

Frankl developed "logotherapy," a psychotherapeutic technique used on patients of trauma to recover their identity. He theorized that the displacement, the horrifying experiences they witnessed, and the tremendous and inconceivable losses robbed people of who they were: their identities, purpose, and future. Frankl believed that psychiatry could help people restore meaning in their lives and open the door to a brighter and more valuable future. He measured success by his patients' increase in hope, and brought back many survivors from the edge of despair.

Unresolved events can make it difficult to move forward and embrace the future you see for yourself. It's like you have one foot on the brake while the other is on the gas. Events that leave scars can lead us to descend into reactive living. This is why learning to *forgive* is perhaps one of the most powerful practices we can employ to realize our vision of the future and achieve our greatness.

Chapter Five

FORGIVE

Hate is heavy, so let it go.

-R.M. Drake

A friend of mine suggested that this chapter be first in the book. A clearing of the decks, so to say. I felt, however, that before you can embrace what is about to unfold in the following pages, you really need to understand the critical role openness plays in making us available to ideas counter to our ego. There are events in our lives that fuel our grievances and it is hard to release injustices and leave them behind. Faith accesses the power of the universe so that we can give up the illusion of control, another important commitment if we are going to get beyond the known and into the unknown. The belief in a future where we are our ideal selves is fuel that drives us to our desired destination based on our actions.

The more emotional baggage we carry, the more difficult our journey forward will be. Unresolved issues will hold us back and weigh us down with a heaviness that makes every step more challenging than it needs to be. As sidewalk poet R.M. Drake said: "Hate is heavy, let it go." Frustratingly, the more we struggle, the deeper we descend into the mire and muck. In this chapter we will learn how to utilize a powerful practice to free our mind and shed the shackles of grievance. The all-powerful practice of forgiveness.

Every person has a space in their mind where anger, disappointment, and rejection reside. This bitter place is filled with memories of the injustices that have done harm to us. Some of these grievances are related to relatively minor, unavoidable events. We can hopefully learn to become better at laughing them off and extending benefit of doubt to those who may have inadvertently offended us. Letting go of those small slights and hurts in close relationships is sometimes difficult, but by talking it through and believing in a common future, we can overcome even these with relative ease. If we can manage to deal with upsetting events quickly, we don't have to carry them with us.

There is another class of hurt that is much more difficult to shed. These incidents include acts of true injustice against our person, acts so hurtful and impactful on our lives that the resulting emotional baggage can be back-breaking. We lug around this huge load every day; we wake up beside it, drag it out of bed in the morning, and we hoist it back up when we go to sleep. Over time, the weight can become crippling.

Whether the hurt is physical, sexual, or emotional—or a combination—and whether it is perpetrated by a parent, teacher, spouse, partner, boss, or schoolyard bully, the impact can have profound long-lasting negative repercussions. These impacts can derail us from becoming our best selves. Indeed, carrying around injustices that take up emotional space in our lives places limits on the relationships we have with others.

Stories of grievances developed around personal violations can be all-consuming and act to color our entire experience of the world. Imagine this scenario: You're driving in wet snow, and slush splatters up onto your windshield. You're out of washer fluid. As the wipers cross your windshield, they smear dirt until it becomes nearly impossible to see out.

It can be terrifying when you can't see where you're going. That is what living with the pain of being wronged feels like. A person drowning in their grievances lives in an almost permanent defensive, reactive state; the feeling of having been wronged is constant and continues to compound. The person cannot help but take every minor event as a personal affront, until these events take up so much emotional bandwidth that there's little room left for focusing on a productive future.

Unfortunately, some people never find a way to get past their personal grievances. Whether their behavioral state manifests itself in anger, fear, or sadness, they have created a cycle where these injustices are the most prominent thing in their lives. The ongoing repetition of this cycle in their minds means that the crime against them is being perpetuated again and again, in relentless perpetuity. Like a parking lot with a "Lot Full" sign, there's literally no room for anything positive, nothing other than this pain, to enter their headspace. *Wouldn't it be nice to be able to tow all those vehicles of pain away to make room for something else?*

On a personal level, this chapter has been difficult for me to write because I know how terribly challenging it is going to be for anyone who has been victimized to imagine a moment where you could let go of the trauma you have experienced. Personal trauma and grievances are very isolating experiences. In deference to that sensitivity, I have used my own past as living proof that where there is a willingness to do so, one can forgive and move on.

I have made reference to a childhood of abuse, and let me be candid. I grew up in a dark place. I was physically and emotionally abused as a young boy and well into my early adolescence. On a daily basis, I experienced this abuse randomly and without provocation. Anything could trigger an event that often quickly escalated into something disproportionately severe. It was the total unpredictability that caused me to live in terror every day. I had no idea where the next blow would come from. It started in my home, and as abuse often does, extended into my wider world. It was as if someone had pinned a permanent "Kick Me" sign to my back. I lived with the stress of fight or flight every single day of my young life.

I don't use the term "abuse" casually. It would be an injustice to all those who have experienced abuse if this subject were treated as perfunctory in this book. It remains difficult for me to talk about this past. I've forged a life separate from it. I feel, however, that the risk of opening myself up in this book is worthwhile if it helps even one person feel that someone else understands.

There is quite simply no excuse for hurting a child. It is such a powerfully insidious act that it perpetuates itself, casting a wider net for predators—who can smell the scent of vulnerability like a shark smells blood from miles away. This is the nature of the beast, and its insidious power means that it is difficult to stop the cycle of abuse. When I was growing up, in the closed circles of the tight-knit community we lived in, talking about abuse was taboo. The community turned a blind eye to what could tarnish its idea of itself and how it was perceived by the outside world. "That sort of thing doesn't happen here," people liked to tell themselves.

Thankfully, today engaging with the subject of abuse has become more mainstream and more open. My dear sweet brother, Rabbi Chaim Ellis, has made combating child abuse an important part of his social work practice. He has shared with me the many presentations he has delivered to the educational community to bring awareness to the topic. He has made it known that abuse in any form is simply unacceptable.

The efforts of people like Chaim save lives. We must not tolerate the instinct to sweep these things under the rug. Anyone who does so becomes complicit in the cycle of abuse. It would make me physically ill to see people within my own community become the subject of "knowing" looks.

> *I am sitting in the Miami airport departure lounge. This woman is berating her young son in front of a crowd waiting to board. "David," she says, grinding her teeth, a quiver in her voice, a wavering finger pointed at him. "You'll see ... what comes around goes around." My stomach painfully churns.*

Abuse is very individual, personal, and painful. Victims too often become isolated by a depreciated sense of self-worth, which subsequently deepens feelings of guilt and the mistaken notion that they bear some responsibility for the abuse. Imagine how a child sees his existence when being raised by an abusive parent who is supposed to protect him. I could not do enough to placate her. I would say and do anything to buy me some time in hopes that she would calm down. If she didn't, my only defense was to retreat into an out-of-body state—where I felt as if I was hovering above painful episodes, looking down, as if the abuse was happening to someone else.

I was severely disciplined. Indiscriminately strapped with a leather belt until I bled, slapped so hard I could really see stars, and regularly told of my worthlessness. I completely dissociated from myself. I can still taste the street salt as I crumpled to the pavement and tried to become one with the tire of a car I fell beside, as my small body endured kicks to my torso. My crime: being a chatty six-year-old. I learned quickly that talking to strangers was unacceptable.

In one flashback, I'm in my underwear, a scrawny, freckled face, thinly boned, completely terrified. I can still see the red indentation on my wrists some 43 years later.

The wire of the power cord rips into my scrawny frame as I struggle from the binding. I am so terrified it is going to completely sever my arms.

I had no idea what I could say to make the abuse stop. She seemed detached, separated from herself. She was out of control. I remember the pain of abandonment, knowing he stood on the other side of that cheaply paneled door. I could not understand why my father did not enter that dimly lit room to stop the madness.

You did not protect me. I realize now that even though it's easier to hate, I have to let it go to become better than I was ever given the chance to be.

The abuse tore through my soul, infected my emotions, tarnished my very being, and robbed me of my childhood. I spent years in cover-up mode, pretending to live a "normal" life. I often felt like an imposter and consistently lived in fear that people would see through me. Eventually, I discovered that forgiveness was foundational to me being able to move on from my past. Without forgiveness, anger eats away and eventually erodes everything creative.

You cannot be your best without letting go of your collection of injustices.

Abuse is often visited upon us by those closest to us, which can create in the abused the most confusing and conflicting of emotions. Simultaneously, we feel at fault, guilty, deserving, ashamed, embarrassed—and alone. These emotions are further magnified in children, who simply cannot comprehend the abuse other than to completely personalize it all. As a result, they develop a crippling sense of emotional inferiority.

A child's view can become so warped by the severe unpredictability of what's taking place outside of their control it can leave deep scarring, a total distrust of everyone and everything, and a complete inability to see the future. A person experiencing this level of mental and physical violation will most certainly suffer serious long-term effects. They become tenants of the place where pain resides. The abused child as an adult can easily and understandably use these feelings of injustice as an excuse to turn to vices to forget or numb their pain.

Abuse leaves a destabilizing and often self-damaging rage in its wake. For someone who experienced this injustice it is incredibly hard to resist dragging that pain with them into new relationships, using it as an excuse to sabotage their potential for love. A person abandoned at birth can carry that sense of rejection with them as an excuse for failure.

Abuse doesn't just affect one life; it often goes on to affect others. People who are abused can find it so ingrained in their psychological construct that they repeat the cycle. The isolation of abuse creates vulnerable victims, who will often turn to a path of self-destruction, suppressing their emotional distress in one way, only for it to surface in another. Dreams unrealized, expectations unmet, passions unfounded, talents under-utilized; this is the legacy of abuse. The effects stretch even further: love, disappointment, anger, and happiness become corrupted, marred, and disfigured. Ongoing pain cheats the victim out of the ability to make sound decisions, and a productive, happy future.

So: *How can we move on from abuse?* Given the emotions and scarring that abuse leaves in its wake, the answer may seem counterintuitive. It is the most difficult practice in these pages— despite the fact that it can be summed up in a single world—and at first glance it may seem like it will do nothing to avenge the pain you feel. It requires all your openness and faith, but it is the only way that I have found to move forward into my future. *Forgiveness.*

But how do you forgive abuse? First and foremost—and most importantly—you must start by realizing that forgiveness is not a gift to the abuser; it is a gift you give to yourself that comes from loving yourself. It is a common misconception that you extend forgiveness to another person. But why would you give anything to someone who has already taken so much from you?! This would only be victimizing yourself further. You need to be the primary beneficiary of your forgiveness. Forgiveness is powerful when you do it for yourself; it will restore your creativity and allow you to embrace a positive future.

> *The unrelenting disappointment in her life seemed to manifest itself in anger towards me. We were five kids at the time living in a small bungalow in midtown Toronto. Chaos reigned. There was no respite from the yelling and screaming. Overwhelmed by the feeling of being denied the life she thought she would have when she walked down the aisle as a beautiful twenty-year-old bride, her dying father looking on, she had just wanted him to be there one last time.*

Forgiveness does not mean that we excuse the actions of those who have hurt us. There is no need to re-assign responsibility. Bringing these events into the open is in itself empowering. Ultimately, the vital realization that releases you from a cycle of pain is that the abuse is not about you. Recognizing abuse is what demystifies it and allows you to take back the power over your future.

The act of empathy is an extension of love, though it is not a prerequisite to forgiveness. I needed to understand my mother's place and time to understand what happened to me. My mother was a product of the 1950s. The Everly Brothers, Buddy Holly, Chuck Berry, Elvis Presley, Little Richard, and Jerry Lee Lewis were all the rage. My mother and her friends were dreamy teenage girls caught up in a time that promised them an exciting future. But when disappointments soon started piling up on her, she couldn't escape the delta between her reality and the ideal life she once dreamed of. I think about a picture that I found in the *Toronto Star*. It's the Santa Claus Parade and my mother is standing on Bloor Street in the crowd holding her little dog and wearing the prettiest hat. She was beautiful, her future in front of her, captured in the click of a shutter.

I have come to recognize that she must have felt herself to be in a seemingly hopeless situation. Neither she nor society at the time, however, had the tools to deal with her feelings. One of the central tenets of the human condition is that we have choice; I eventually came to recognize that the choices she made came out of a place of brokenness. That day, so many years later, when she drew me close, her body decimated from chemo and radiation, she mouthed that she was sorry. I finally understood the tragedy of her life. Later, I would sometimes weep at her grave. Crying for what could have been.

I am now 13 years older than she was when she died. As I reflect on my own maturation, I have to believe that had she lived longer she too would have experienced similar growth. I mourn the opportunity she missed.

> *Forgiveness is about coming to a place where I can move my life forward. Life is not about anger, but rather intense love. For what greater demonstration of love is there than the pursuit of understanding and making peace so her memory could rest well?*

A precondition for forgiveness is to relinquish the obsession with grieving. Why do we obsess if it is clear that our obsession sustains the hurtful cycle that our abusers started? This question speaks to the power abuse has over our being. When we are unable to reconcile the injustices we experienced, we return to them over and over again. What is worse, over time, is that we can start to take a sort of unconscious pleasure in returning to an obsession that wreaks havoc on our lives. Bergler calls this "injustice collecting." Neatly stacked in our emotional closets, our injustices give us comfort and provide us with excuses when we fall short of reaching our potential.

As long as we allow the past to victimize us, we will continue to collect and hoard real and imagined injustices that perpetuate our self-destruction. For those of us feeling regret or anger, there is no limit to the imagined injustices we can find. It can even get to a point where we lose sight of what is justified and what is imagined. When we face a setback, we stand at the center of a fulcrum; with our next move, we will tip one way or the other, either towards personalizing what has happened or giving way to granting the benefit of the doubt.

Living with a sense of injustice tilts us towards taking things personally and limits our ability to see things differently. When we fail to take responsibility for our choices and own our lives, the creativity within us lies dormant—and with it the potential to realize what we can achieve. It is not until we recognize this pattern and the twisted pleasure we derive from it that we can fight back and break the cycle. Not reaching our potential drives us into regret, where age and the passing of time only deepens the power of the injustice committed against us, either real or perceived. It's like scar tissue that accumulates over time. The earlier we can deal with it and break it down, the better.

I used to think of the pattern of injustice collecting every time I heard the outgoing message on cousin Geoff's voicemail in the period leading up to the last difficult year of his life: *Sorry, I'm not here to take your call, and if this is Cecil (his father), you can just [expletive] off!*

His message made me sad. Here was an intelligent, loving, and giving person who just could not bring himself to even approach forgiveness. I was pretty close to it all—our families were linked by the same sickness—and what he felt about his father was more than justified, but it was so sad to see that he could not let it go.

That hate followed him as he battled AIDS and sunk deeper into despair. In the end, the EMS resuscitated him in an alleyway in Vancouver's infamous East End only to have him die in some emergency corridor alone. It wasn't the disease that killed him, but rather the vices he turned to, to fill a void he could not deal with. *Why did someone with such promise go so wildly off track?* Because for all of his genius and creativity he could not find the means to forgive, and by maintaining his hate he disavowed responsibility for his own life.

It is easy to allow ourselves to be trapped in cycles where every affront is seen as a personal attack. An attack can be as simple as a running refrain of *why me?*

The antidote to this type of mindset, however, is to be mindful of feeling victimized. Practicing the exercise of giving the "benefit of the doubt" is an excellent proactive way to defuse feelings of being targeted. If you are challenged and blockaded by something that has started to fester and occupy space in your mind, it is going to come at a cost to those you love and to who you want to become. Let it go. Find the space to forgive. The payoff is your personal growth. Getting past injustices is a huge positive accelerator.

⌒⌒

Repressing personal injustices locks you into a self-limiting emotional place. To move forward, your only recourse is to bring injustices out into the open. It takes time to acknowledge what has happened, to come to terms with it, and to seek the best way forward. To move on, you must "feel" ready. The good news is that there are clearly defined steps you can take to guide you.

Of the books I have read on the subject of forgiveness, those that stand out for me include *Man's Search for Meaning* by Viktor Frankl (1946); *Making Peace with Your Parents* by Harold Bloomfield M.D. (1983); the various writings of Erich Fromm; and the works of Edmund Bergler. One of the most practical texts I have read was *Forgive for Good* by Dr. Fred Luskin (2001). These authors greatly influenced my quest to understand myself and my needs, and to make peace with my own past.

In particular, Luskin's book breaks down the process of forgiveness into three important steps. He says the first step is to recognize our feelings of hurt. By this, he is referring to the need to recognize that we were wronged and that what happened to us was unjust and undeserved, and that it is important for us to acknowledge the effect this injustice has had on our lives. The idea is to allow yourself to feel angry, or vulnerable, or sad. By consciously allowing emotions to surface, you recognize that you are entitled to them; in doing so, you can take back the control that was lost when the injustice occurred. One of the most hurtful things incurred by any injustice is the degrading feeling that comes from the removal of control over our life. An injustice can feel like a violation of our independence and self-worth.

It wasn't really until I was in my 30s that I could "admit" that I was a victim of abuse. I emphasize the word "admit" because it implies wrong-doing and guilt, which is actually what a victim of abuse may feel: *She would beat me because I was a bad kid! I must have been very bad.*

I first started to acknowledge and talk about my own abuse as I began to watch my own kids grow up. I saw a reflection of myself in my son Eitan. I was about the same age when the abuse really got out of hand. Looking at the innocence, vulnerability, neediness, and beautifulness of this child caused a renewed anger at my treatment at this age. How could a parent do such a thing?! The memories of what I endured started to unearth themselves, and there I was, as a young father, seeing my past for the first time. Serendipitously, at this time, I came across the book *A Man Named Dave* (1999), by Dave Pelzer. As a child, Dave was abused by his alcoholic mother, and his journey to forgiveness inspired me. To this point, I had never even realized that I had the option to forgive.

The next step, Luskin asserts, is to depersonalize the actions perpetuated against you. This is not an easy task! It is natural to think of injustices done to us as personal attacks and to project the damage inwards. When we do this, however, we incorrectly take responsibility for something that someone else has done to us. *Is it the child's fault that a parent has abused them? Of course not!*

When you are victimized, it is easy to feel singled out and targeted. The reality is that it was not, in fact, about you and could just have easily been someone else. You need to stop taking responsibility for what has happened to you and put the blame firmly where it belongs. When we make the injustice solely about ourselves, it is impossible to see our way clear of it.

It was spring of 2005. I was walking along a street in my neighborhood and met a guy in front of this large home unloading a trailer into his garage. The scene was a bit out of context, and we started to talk. I was immediately enamored with him and we became fast friends. Very soon after, we went into business together. We started to make some serious money importing one of the first miniature digital cameras. Gerry was a charmer. He would bring flowers to my wife almost weekly and always had a little something for my mother-in-law, who, it would turn out, was justly wary of him. He would come flying into the office like Aladdin on a magic carpet, and everyone would bask in his light.

But alas, Gerry's real business was stealing. He had been fraudulently redirecting funds from customers into his own bank accounts and siphoning money from the company. Over a period of few months, he ended up stealing $250,000 from us.

When I discovered his fraud and confronted him, he had the audacity to account for his actions by saying, "God delivered you to me." As if I was sent to him by some divine providence so he could use me to serve his own ends. I almost fell over. It became clear that the guy couldn't help himself. It didn't matter that he would have made far more money if he had been honest with me. He was not just a thief; he was pathological.

What rankled me the most, however, was not just the stolen money, but the betrayal of my trust. It sent me spiraling into depression. Deep down, I knew the real pain came from the knowledge that Gerry had seen something in me he could take advantage of. He had purposely chosen me as his victim and manipulated me.

I eventually came to learn that I was not his only victim. Knowing that gave me some comfort that it was not personal—but I could never be sure. It was as if he knew that the stupidity we felt would override any pursuit for justice. Like the others, I just wanted to put the whole sordid affair behind me. I had no doubt that Gerry would ultimately receive his comeuppance, but I wanted no part in it.

Eventually the day came when I got up and stopped feeling sorry for myself. I depersonalized the situation. And once I did, I went on to make several times the money we had made during our short time together. I created a lucrative import and distribution business. Those enterprises led me into the warehousing business and eventually to becoming the CEO of AdvancePro.

None of that would have happened had I focused solely on revenge, thereby victimizing myself by refusing to forgive and move on. In fact, I came to realize I owed this pitiful bastard some gratitude for pushing me down that path. Eliasz, my wife's grandfather, coined the phrase "the *Shvartz* factor," in reference to a business partner with the last name of Schwartz who stole from their underground shoe manufacturing business in Poland. We used to joke about it once I was able to put Gerry's betrayal behind me. "Beware of the *Shvartz*," he would say, winking at me.

My main advice to anyone reading this book: If you identify a Gerry—trust your feelings, turn around, and walk far away. Do not let a bigger-than-life personality fool you. Investigate objectively who you are about to deal with. If your intuition flashes warning lights, pay attention.

The third step in the process of forgiveness is to find a trusted person who will allow you to tell them your story of grievance.

I was 13 years old when I met Chai Taub. Her husband, Dovid, brought me home after we met on a dreary, snowy Montreal day. We both walked into a bakery off Van Horne at the same time; I was despondent and off in my own world, which Dovid noticed. We fell into a conversation and for some reason I blurted out the misery of my life. Sitting on their couch on Ave de Vimy in Montreal clutching one of Chai's colored pillows for dear life, it was the first time I felt safe to speak.

I had been shipped off to a religious parochial school where I was alone, despite the fact that I was there with my brother. We responded to the rigidity and demand for religious conformity differently. He became distant and hard. I felt like he abandoned me in the time of my greatest need in favor of the security conformity provided. I knew of the trauma nested within him from the past we shared. I called out the hypocrisy of those in charge of me. I hated my years in that wretched place, having been sent away because of "the sickness in the *heim* (home)." God forbid someone should say the word "cancer" out aloud, which was what was killing my mother.

In my darkest hours of need, Chai threw me a life vest. For over two years I would come and visit her to unload my feelings and hurt. I wasn't the only one; this saintly woman helped so many of us lost boys. Looking back, we were easy to identify, the emotionally wrecked and vulnerable. What I learned from Chai is that by showing some kindness and providing a listening ear, you can change the course of someone's life. I have never forgotten how important she was to me, to find someone to trust and to be able to tell my story without fear of reprisal. I am forever thankful to her in ways that cannot be expressed.

When we first met, I was very afraid of revealing too much of my difficult history to my wife, Limore. I thought for sure she would see me as damaged goods and take off running. As we began to get to know one another, I had to continually pinch myself to confirm that I was not dreaming, that someone could actually love me. The idea of sharing everything you are with another person was foreign to me growing up. It took me some time to realize that I had found not just a wife, but my most trusted and truest friend. The first time we went out we talked for hours, about everything, but it would take years for the real minutia to start coming out.

When it did, she listened patiently and without judgment. Twenty-five plus years later, she still does. I am not the easiest person to get along with; the past resurfaces from time to time in unpredictable ways, but I have learned to be comfortable with my own vulnerability. Having that unconditional love has been foundational to me to come to a place of forgiveness.

It is important to be able to vent and talk about our feelings and emotions. As social creatures, we gain strength and perspective from our interactions with others, especially those that counteract those more harmful relationships. The trick of telling your story and its attendant grievances is not to stop with the terrible things that have happened, but to insistently continue the narrative as you become a hero in your own story.

A point of caution here: Stories of grievance have a shelf life. There is a point of repetition where you risk becoming a broken record. No one has the patience to listen to the same grievance over and over again. Grievances can also eventually manifest themselves to include things that did not happen. People who have chosen to dedicate their lives to bearing crosses often become so obsessed that they lose the connection to what really happened.

Don't become trapped in this cycle. You get a limited number of passes before your story of grievance needs to evolve into one of "heroism"—and this is the story you can tell over and over again. No one gets tired of hearing about heroism. It is motivating and positive. A story of overcoming hardship gives strength to others, and every hero deserves to share their story.

Peter Silverman was only 17 when the Nazis swept into Poland. He survived the Holocaust by escaping into the woods and joining a small group of Jewish resistance fighters who fought back, a story he recounted in his memoir *From Victims to Victors* (1992). While just a teen, this unassuming man took matters into his own hands. He refused to be a victim. I was very fortunate to have had many conversations with him. What impressed me most was his ability to take the most unimaginable injustice and survive it to become a victor in his story.

A positive ending to a story can be a huge confidence builder. As you recognize your ability to overcome, you unleash your creative potential. When you talk about things that have happened in the past, make sure to explain how you would prefer to see your life unfold. Talk about your goals and how you are going to achieve them, despite that event.

The words of an acquaintance recovering from a bad relationship are instructive here: "I know I can have a great relationship with someone and I have learned to really appreciate the importance of love after the hell I went through in my first marriage." Following this advice, when I talk about my past, I make sure to go beyond the abuse I went through to where I am today. I talk about my wife and children and the life I have built. I want people to know me by my successes, not pity me for my past. You need to define yourself as the hero in your story, because when you do, your story of grievance will become one of strength and success.

Forgiveness was one of my greatest challenges and it has been one of my most rewarding achievements. And it has paid off big time. I am now a loving husband and father. I am a better friend and a confident businessman. There will always be triggers that bring me back to the hurt of my childhood and cause me to act reactively, but forgiveness has allowed me to take back my agency and forge a path forward—where that injustice does not define me. Life is too short to hold on to grievances.

Forgiveness is an ongoing activity. When we find ourselves harboring hurt and resentment, there are a couple of key practices we can use to let go and move forward.

The practice of "active love" is particularly effective when you get angry with someone close to you. I find I can remove the feeling of blame and prevent myself from obsessing over who is wrong or right if I instead make myself think about the things I love about that person. Note that while this may not necessarily solve the immediate situation, it removes tension and brings perspective so that we can both move to a more rational place and have a conversation, rather than an ego-laden confrontation.

This act is the gateway to unconditional love. A close relationship can easily breed co-dependence and judgment. Feeling responsibility for someone close to you can lead to complex feelings, be it a close friend, sibling, child, or spouse; you may feel that you have a say in how they "ought" to live their lives. Without realizing it, you have started to exert some kind of control, and when the person refuses to submit to that control, it can leave you feeling rejected.

Allow yourself to draw a line in the sand and cede responsibility for the life choices of others. Put all your efforts into practicing active love and become mindful of the positive things you love about the people in your life. You may find that all the negatives that might potentially be divisive will fade away. As the illusion of control disappears, you are then left with unconditional love.

Like forgiveness, active love is something you do for yourself. While I can offer love to someone, it does not mean it will be returned. That's okay. By offering it and expecting nothing in return, I have allowed myself to let go. Through understanding, depersonalizing the actions of others, and being unconditional, you protect yourself from anyone taking advantage of you. Feelings of responsibility become normalized, devoid of guilt and judgment. All these things can now have a positive impact on your creative process and thereby increase your potential.

Another powerful relationship practice that works in combination with active love is providing your partner with the "benefit of the doubt." When you couple this with active love, there is little that can divide you, assuming both parties are invested in the relationship. The consistent provision of the benefit of doubt is no easy task, however.

In the moment something goes wrong, it is easy to regress into an injustice-collecting state of mind and fulfill your immediate emotional desire to find fault in others. Finding fault is the path of least resistance for your ego. It allows you to feel that whatever just took place is about you, when it fact it could have nothing to do with you.

One time, my business partner and I were getting out of a taxi after a long flight and the driver did not bother to assist us with our luggage; he just opened the trunk. As we were standing on the curb outside our hotel, I made a comment about the lack of assistance. Jason responded by suggesting, "Maybe he has a disability." It was a simple idea that may or may not have been the case, but to think that way immediately removed any minor injustice I might have been feeling. That is the empathy that is facilitated when we provide others with the benefit of the doubt. When you practice this, you stop personalizing perceived injustice, and "poof" it just goes away. What a much better way to live!

Empathy, active love, unconditional love, and giving the benefit of the doubt all lead to our ability to depersonalize and forgive. The great thing about these practices is that they do not require an active partner. These are individual practices that you do for yourself. If you have a willing partner who participates in these practices, albeit in their own way, then that is great. If not, it does not affect the outcome for you. It is up to you to decide what relationship you want with others, and how you react when things get tough.

Sometimes, however, the hardest person to forgive is yourself. When I mess up, I am really affected by it. I hate it when the people around me make avoidable mistakes, but nothing makes me crazier than when I make my own. I don't always manage to find perspective in those moments, and instead bury myself deeper. In situations like these, it is vital to be able to apply the principles of active love to yourself. It hurts to have no one else to blame, but it's okay to extend the same generosity to yourself as you do to others. Give yourself a pass.

Emotional hurt or even recalling a hurt can easily manifest itself as a physical pain. I was recently at a dinner party and I ran into someone who told me he grew up on the same street as my family. "With all the kids. Right?" he said. "Wasn't your mother sick? What happened to all you guys?" I started to respond, but as I got into it, I felt a heat rise in my chest and up through my throat, spreading across my rib cage and into my stomach. I recognized that my body was telling me it was not a healthy conversation to have, and so I changed the topic to something more recent.

Throughout my childhood and into my adolescence, I suffered from severe cramping. So much so that I would often double over in pain, unable to walk. There was no medical explanation, which led to accusations that I was simply seeking attention. In the end I was often derided as "the little boy who cried wolf." The truth is, I had a severe unexplainable physical pain almost all the time, somewhere in my body. It was only when I started going through the process of forgiveness that these symptoms abated. Forgiveness freed me not just from emotional pain, but from physical pain as well.

Here is a meditative practice that I find helpful to counter the effect of physical pain that can originate from emotional triggers. Start a breath from your belly. Recognizing that your heart is where your feelings reside, place your hands gently over your heart as you breathe. This act should give you a feeling of protection and care. With each breath, allow the muscles and ligaments protecting your organs to relax. Now, imagine a pure white light entering into your mind; let it wash through you. Next, imagine a trapdoor in the back of your head; open it to allow the light to exit, taking with it all your thoughts, leaving your mind clean and open. Continue deep, conscious breaths as you let the light come into your shoulders. Relax your shoulders by pushing them down and away from your ears. The light will now continue by extending through your arms and fingers before making its way back up through your throat to be exhaled.

Breathe in the light one more time; this time imagine you are breathing in the source of pure life into your body and allow it to pass through your midsection, wrapping itself around your heart and your organs before traveling through your groin and each leg, and then back up again. Exhale. Each time you breathe, think of the light entering your body, and each time you exhale let it take with it all the diseased, damaged, and dark bits. You should now start to feel everything in your body relax.

Now think about everything you are grateful for in your life, and all the gifts you have. When you are done, the pain you feel will have subsided, or even have disappeared completely, and you will feel refreshed and strong.

This practice takes just a few minutes and can be practiced anywhere, at any time. I have found it an extremely effective method for washing out the negative and replacing it with the positive, the ideal mindset for forgiveness.

In his book *Making Peace with Your Parents*, Bloomfield suggests another technique for fostering forgiveness: writing a letter you may never deliver. Confronting someone does not always work out well, as it will often result in a defensive reaction. Most people who play a role in the circle of abuse make every situation about them. Often the person who has committed an injustice against you has moved on in some way or another, and is no longer available to you. How do you confront them then?

During my 30s, I was having a conversation with my father when he shifted into some delusional, nostalgic dialogue related to his good parenting. I knew that I was not going to make headway in this conversation or with my grievance. He would never admit to his role. He has never apologized or taken any form of responsibility. Instead, any conversation of our past focuses on how bad it was for him.

You'll never win an argument against a narcissist because they'll never be able to see any perspective but their own. So I wrote him a letter that I will never deliver. It allowed me to say what I needed to say. Remember, forgiveness is for you alone; no one else needs to be part of that process. Sure, recognition—for example, an apology—has its place and meaning, but to what end? *How will that change the past?* I am the only one who can release me from my past.

Forgiveness unlocks your potential by releasing the blockages that impede your emotional health and creativity. As soon as you give someone else that power, they are back in control and you are once again dependent and a victim. You must own your power in the same way you get to own your forgiveness.

I had a friend who would write a letter every time he felt "screwed" by the system. Some letters would go out, others would not. Sometimes, he even got responses. Validation wasn't the only reason he wrote the letter. He needed to express his feelings and emotional state.

Bloomfield's practice is very powerful. Try it. Write a letter to someone you can no longer confront, even if you wanted to, and read it aloud. Feel the release and let the injustice go. Allow yourself to forgive.

There is a shadow that follows me around. He has a scrawny, freckled face, and he is hollowed, unsure, tepid, and scared. I am ashamed of him; he sits there and he reminds me of someone I used to know. Usually, I can only see him out of the corner of my eye. I don't want anyone else to see him. It would be humiliating. For most of my adult life, I'd pretend he wasn't there. Until one day I gently invited him to come and sit beside me and to share in all the glory that we accomplished together.

I realized that I had abandoned him and left him shivering alone to manage an eternity of pain. How could I do such a thing? Me, of all people? Was I so callous as to try and forget where I came from? Am I so embarrassed? He wants nothing from me except my attention, love, and understanding. After all, he has been through it all. He is a big part of my life. He is me. And so now he sits proudly beside me and we are in this together. He's no longer scrawny, and I'm no longer ashamed. Together we are completed, we are strong, and we are a force to be reckoned with.

We all have a shadow of ourselves. Don't hide them; bring them into the open. It's because of your shadow that you are who you are today.

The act of inviting your shadow—that internal version of yourself that you most associate with some shame and/or pain—into your life provides incredible benefits. I was once doing business with someone who intimidated me. He would make me feel small every time he was around. I would lose my words and my confidence would erode. Then one day, I invited my shadow to join me and everything changed. All of a sudden, I realized he could not succeed in making me feel less than the confident and capable person I had become, because next to me, sitting right up front, was my partner, the scared kid I was. The best thing about this realization is that instead of having a confrontation, I received respect and he engaged with my total presence. Our relationship improved and the noise was gone so that our business could proceed without any distraction.

Terrible things happen all the time in the world. When we have empathy, it's hard to face the violence and hatred we see around us. I stood quietly outside the Café Bonne Biere in the 11th district of Paris on November 14th, 2015, just one day after 160 people were murdered in three separate terrorist attacks. The flowers and candles were just starting to collect. I didn't know anyone affected, but I remember feeling numb and a sense of disbelief. I was overcome by the senseless injustice and cowardice of the terrorist attack. My faith was shaken. *How do we find forgiveness in our hearts?* I wondered as I stood there and openly cried. The answer came to me months later.

June 12, 2016, marked the worst mass shooting in US history at the time. Forty-nine people were gunned down in Pulse nightclub in Orlando, Florida. One of the fallen victims was Mercedez Marisol Flores; her father, while being interviewed by CNN, said the following: "I forgive the boy because I cannot take that hate in my life. My life is more important than hate." With that simple statement, he gave me the answer I was looking for.

Even after experiencing the most horrific thing that could happen to a father, he chose forgiveness. He wasn't going to perpetuate this violence and hate; he was going to defy it with courage and light. I honestly do not know how many of us could muster this kind of poetic resolve in this most tragic of circumstances. I pray that Mr. Flores has found that peace. He sent a very powerful and positive message out into the world in response to what was probably the worst moment of his life. He has my respect and admiration.

Flores's father underscores the final point I want to make about forgiveness. Don't wait for someone to acknowledge you've forgiven them; don't expect to be the provider of absolution. As I started the process of coming to terms with my childhood, I began a personal campaign. I called my former principal from my elementary school; I was angry with him that he did not intercede. "Yes, (heavy sigh), I remember you," he said. "I don't know what to say, it was a different time." I heard an old man on the phone who had his own problems to deal with and suddenly his response did not matter as much. I did not need to confront him; he was not that person. *It was a different time.* I felt a release, I forgave.

I called my Aunt Ruth, the widow of my father's brother, someone whom I had maybe spoken to a handful of times. She did not feign surprise at the call. She did not skip a beat. In a firm, prickly, and impatient voice, her response was cold and to the point. "Look, let me give you some advice," she said. "Move on and get over it." Then she hung up. End of conversation.

At the time, her dismissal hurt; it felt like yet again someone was telling me that I didn't matter. But then in the same instant I realized that I didn't need her to tell me anything; it was my responsibility to take this action for myself. And this is perhaps what forgiveness is really about: making the decision to live our best lives for ourselves, not for others. When we do this, we can shed the weight of what was, to enable us to deal with what is. The act of forgiveness is all about you. Do it for yourself. Let it go. Move on. Triumph!

PART II

IN THE PURSUIT OF GREATNESS

Chapter Six

FUEL YOUR CONFIDENCE

*If we all did the things we are capable of doing, we would
literally astound ourselves.*

-Thomas Alva Edison

The last four chapters have dealt with the four foundations for building a healthy personal structure. These are the prerequisites to achieving your greatness. Choosing to be open, ceding control and having faith, believing in your future, and allowing yourself to forgive. Following these principles will help you modify your beliefs and accept new truths that will in turn motivate you to take actions that will lead you to becoming your best self. By following these steps, you move the bar for both what is expected of you (from yourself and others) and for what you believe is possible. You leave behind mediocrity in the pursuit of personal greatness.

Having come through these chapters together, we are now ready to look deeper within as we start to put what we have learned into practice. There is a place where consciousness, belief, and intuition intersect to embolden the faith we have in ourselves to enable us to take the actions necessary to optimize our lives going forward. This is *confidence*.

Your confidence is your faith at work. You accept that not everything is within your control and that there is a higher power that will deliver. But you also understand that this deliverance is dependent on you taking actions that will give you the best opportunity to achieve your dreams. It is your confidence that gives you the strength and audacity to move through walls.

Every action we take is directly related to our confidence. The more we value ourselves and the healthier our intuition, the greater the chance we will act in our own best interests. Self-confidence is related to our sense of agency and will drive the decisions we make. Ultimately, there is only one captain of your ship. The choices you make are yours and yours alone.

Confidence is self-perpetuating—a living perpetual motion machine. It creates its own momentum: confidence breeds success, which breeds more confidence, and in turn more success. Through this feedback loop, confidence keeps opening us up to newer and greater possibilities, transforming wants into needs, and needs into realities. In this way, confidence is power. Power generated from within.

Confidence is a product of two things: the emotional feelings we have about our sense of self-worth; and self-efficacy, a conscious assessment of our competence to achieve things. How we view and feel about ourselves is going to have a major impact on our self-confidence, which is affected by how well equipped we are to deal with our personal history and the gaps we identify between our real and ideal selves. Our confidence is also built through positive achievements; the more we accomplish and grow, the greater our momentum.

One of the lingering after-effects of abuse, the systematic attack on your sense of self, is that you stop trusting yourself. Every action, every decision, is accompanied by a fear of being punished or hurt. When you live with abuse, you are never sure what's about to come or how your actions will be interpreted. As a result, you lack even the most basic confidence that most people access without thinking: the faith that certain actions will produce certain outcomes, that you know what will happen in the next five minutes, and that you can deal with it. In this light, I guess you could say that when it came to confidence, I started out at ground zero.

You do not need to be a victim of abuse to suffer from a lack of confidence. Some people naturally struggle with a surplus of self-doubt. This struggle can make it difficult to take action, to advocate for what we need, or to take ownership over decisions. The reality is that almost everyone has moments when their confidence is challenged. During an episode of self-doubt, it takes a great deal of fortitude not to let the situation intimidate and control us. Self-doubt is like kryptonite to Superman; it siphons off self-confidence and leaves us feeling weakened and reduced. The trick is to recognize when our confidence is compromised and to quickly find a place of safe refuge within, where we can figure things out before we react.

One thing to remember is that no one can see the self-doubt inside us. Until I figure out what is destabilizing my confidence, I try to keep a good poker face. This is sometimes easier said than done, especially when a situation occurs unexpectedly. Here is a practice you can try. Let's say you are in a predicament of your own making; for example, getting clocked for speeding. As the officer approaches your car, internally recognize your culpability. You will find that this will help you regain power over the situation. In fact, admitting responsibility will actually give you self-confidence and allow you to avoid shrinking guiltily under the gaze of the traffic cop.

On two separate occasions I was pulled over on the same stretch of Highway 416 while driving my daughter back to school in Ottawa. As soon as I pulled to the side and could see the officer making his way over, I made the conscious decision to accept the outcome. "Yes, officer," I said. "I recognize I was speeding. I doubt the reason is important to you, so I won't go there." I smiled. "I only ask, if you don't mind, to make it as painless as possible." In each instance, the officer was very understanding, and in one case I was let off with a warning.

Once I was able to regain my self-confidence, I could speak from a place of power that projected itself outward. I knew that no matter what the outcome of the interaction was, I would be okay. A speeding ticket is, of course, minor, but the lesson isn't. Instead of allowing your self-depreciating energy to take over and reduce you to a shadow of yourself, by being honest with yourself, you can regain the control and confidence you need to resolve almost any situation.

The same technique can be used in situations where we cannot control the narrative. For example, it is inevitable that at some point we will encounter a bully who has a talent for intimidation. Early on in my business career I failed miserably when I encountered people like this, because I tended to take everything personally. I cared so much about what I was doing; anything negative felt like a personal attack. I did exactly what the other side predicted, and they would play me like a puppet. Finally, I learned how to depersonalize the situation and get back into control.

There are techniques you can use to build a force field to protect you from those who are skilled at touching a nerve. Prior to walking into meetings, I now make it a habit to ask myself the most important questions: *What do I want to happen here? What is the goal of this meeting?* Keeping my eye on the endgame often masks any scent of vulnerability, and I find that I can disarm almost any situation by being proactive and staying focused.

Focus on what you "need" to happen, rather what you "want" to happen. Your wants can be influenced by unmet needs from Maslow's hierarchy, and pursuing them can unconsciously expose you to emotional minefields set by people who would take advantage of you. As always, it is important to beware the pleasure-pain pattern; even if we are not aware of it, we may be attracted to that minefield, knowing the pain it holds.

By recognizing when we are tempted to do something against our own self-interest, we can avoid situations that will sap our confidence.

People are afraid to pursue their most important dreams, because they feel that they don't deserve them, or that they'll be unable to achieve them.

-Paulo Coelho

How often have you decided you are not capable of doing something before you've even tried to do it? The truth is that most of us live with a great deal of self-doubt because we fear failure so much. Where confidence represents a belief in ourselves, fear is the opposite; it's our disbelief in ourselves. While confidence is the source of positive energy that helps us grow, learn, and change, fear is an instinctive, unconscious, and reactive force that takes our control away.

Don't get me wrong, fear has its place. It is a vital and natural, often instinctive, response to the physical and emotional dangers we face—if we didn't feel it, we couldn't protect ourselves from legitimate threats. But it is not this instinctive, hair-raising fear I am talking about here.

The fear I want to talk about is the nemesis of self-confidence, and like confidence it breeds upon itself, becoming more powerful as it takes root. Instinctive and unavoidable, it wages war on decisiveness, stymies objectivity, and starves our creativity. Fear knows no boundaries; it is that anxiety-laden feeling that visits us in the middle of the night leaving us chilled from sweats, even on the warmest of evenings. It's that feeling that starts out as butterflies in our gut and as it builds, lodges itself in the base of our throat. I get a twitching right eyelid—which drives me crazy. Whatever form it takes, fear can be suffocating; it demands total surrender, paralyzing our body and mind. Once unleashed, it chokeholds confidence and can drag us down into a reactive hell.

Like confidence, fear is power, but it is power that takes from the world, not power that gives back. It's the "dark side of the force." Combating something so primal and immediate isn't easy, but it can be done. In fact, it must be done. When we don't manage fear, it can become prophetic. For example, when the media engages in fear-mongering about a slowing economy, consumer and corporate spending decreases, even if there are no real reasons for it. Over and over again, we have experienced self-induced collapses of systems that have started with the fear of that same collapse. People and companies trade on fear; insurance, while important, uses fear to oversell the occurrence of the unlikely and the unknown. I remember the first time Limore and I talked to a friend in the life insurance business; throughout the conversation he kept referring to her directly as "the widow." I was like, *Hello, I'm still here!* For months after, we would hesitantly joke about it, as if we were worried talking about it could be prophetic.

When people trade on your fears, what they are really doing is distracting you and changing your decision-making process from an objective one to an emotional, reactive one. As a rule, I simply cut off the conversation when I realize someone is trying to use fear to sell me something. Needless to say, though we did eventually get life insurance, we did not get it from the widow-maker.

> *Does anyone see my fear? Sometimes I have to take a look in the mirror just to reassure myself that they can't. It's easy to let fear gain momentum, but challenging our fears directly is necessary to maintaining self-confidence.*

I'll let you in on a secret. I live in the grip of fear every day. Some fears I experience are rational; they are about finances, sales, investment risks, etc. These would be fairly normal, everyday types of fears. Others are less rational: *It's 5:15PM, my kid's not home yet. I haven't heard from my wife. Any moment there will be a knock on the door.* You get the idea. We all have thoughts that pop into our heads that we would never speak of; these only become a problem when they consume us and then we may definitely want to seek help to bring them back under control.

Every day I triage situations that come up on the fly, and I can get stuck in episodes of self-doubt that creep up on me just as I am about to take a decisive action. As a leader, I have to be confident in my abilities and my judgment. It can be dangerous for people who must make snap judgments and decisions to lose their confidence. I remember our obstetrician, Dr. Rosman, expertly lifting the umbilical cord that was wrapped around our youngest son's neck as he was being born; I cannot imagine the doctor doubting himself at that critical moment. Confidence is necessary for us to be able to assess a set of inputs in the flash of a moment and to then act appropriately. That's why it is so important to challenge and root out any fear that might stifle it.

To root out fear, we must first recognize it for what it really is. We need to demystify fear, bring it out in the open, and face it head on. We can start by recognizing that fear is a natural response to things we cannot control. It's okay to feel anxious about taking action, whether it's launching a business, giving a speech, or embarking on something new. I have spoken in public many times, and there is not once, when the room quietens, that I do not experience fear, anxiety, and doubt. I've learned to rein in my fear by reassuring myself that I have done this before and that I know what I am doing. If anything, fear in these moments can be a humbling force.

There is a simple breathing exercise that can help to offset anxiety created by fear. Breathe deeply through your nose and focus on the air coming in and out of your lungs. Inhale and count to seven. Exhale and count to eleven. This kind of controlled breathing engages the parasympathetic nervous system, which comes online and counters our sympathetic nervous system's fight or flight response to daily stresses. This mindfulness practice brings our internal discourse back to rational thoughts and feelings. By quieting the physical symptoms of fear, we return to measured responses.

Fear tends to blow things out of proportion. When I start to feel overwhelmed, I find that breaking things down into their smallest parts and then creating steps to achieving the endgame goes a long way to de-stressing. Make a needs list, mind map, and verbalize your feelings. Break down your list into sublists of smaller steps. The more detailed your list, the less fearful and more in control you will feel. Take the mystery out of an action or decision, and fear loses much of its power over you. Creating detailed lists of action items can also be a great motivator and confidence booster. With every item you strike off, you gain momentum and your confidence increases.

As an entrepreneur I deal with a diverse set of roles and range of activities. I'm on my unicycle spinning a bunch of plates at the same time. From being in business to co-running a busy household, there is a daily list of things I have to get done. Lists keep me centered, and every time I get to cross off an item, I feel empowered. I mentioned earlier that the act of writing is visceral and goes a long way to making things real and within reach. Writing puts things in front of us to see, and puts them out into the universe.

It's early morning on the first day of the New Year and I find myself awake in the early hours, overwhelmed by what faces me in the year ahead. My personal and professional commitments. The milestones I want to achieve. Everything that goes into raising (and paying for!) four kids. A great deal hinges on my ability to be successful, and under that pressure, fear and anxiety start to tighten their grip on me. I get out of bed and open a clean spreadsheet on my computer. I close my eyes against the glow of the computer screen and when I open them again, I give myself a moment to gaze out the window at the light edging over the horizon, above swaying palm trees and the glassy, still, inter-coastal waters. In that moment, I think about how grateful I am to have these challenges, and I say a silent prayer of thanks.

To remove the edge from my anxiety, I breathe deeply; I acknowledge that I can only do what I can do. I think back to all that I have accomplished before, and this puts me in an optimistic state of mind. I remind myself that I am loved and part of a universe that delivers good things when they are meant to be. I then identify all the things on my mind this morning and consciously acknowledge them as "goals." I go back to my computer and break down each in its own spreadsheet. I start by looking at the details of each goal, building a task list, adding financial details, and considering any risk associated with it.

When the individual goal sheets are done, I move on to a master plan that lays out my capital outflow requirements against my projected financial inflow. I can now look at the numbers and the effect on asset value opportunity. My work is cut out for me, but by the time I am done, I have converted this feeling of being overwhelmed into something I can see and grasp, something tangible I can now work with.

The result is that I am back in control, and instead of being mired in negative, regressive feelings of anxiety that attack my confidence, my creativity kicks into high gear and I become excited at the challenges that lay ahead. After only a couple of hours of work, I can sit back and grasp the overall plan. I have a precise knowledge of what my needs are in order to get this all done. I have cleared my head, and now what's on my mind is to get the most out of the day ahead with my family. It's time to send those needs out into the universe ... and I think we'll head to the beach.

The most amazing thing about overcoming fear is not just that it allows you to regain your confidence, but that the very act is itself a confidence accelerator. This speaks to the power of confidence to reinforce itself and create its own momentum, turning a spiral of fear and darkness into a blossoming of faith and light.

There are a number of daily practices you can use to keep your confidence healthy and thriving. One is to revisit past successes. I've spoken to this already, but it's worth repeating. The practice of recounting your positive achievements is very powerful, especially when faced with fear or doubt. By looking back on your past accomplishments, you are confirming that you are capable and able to reach your goals and succeed. There is a mounted picture in my office of my team at the base of the CN Tower in the first days of Cybermind. I call it *The Breakfast Club* picture, named after the 1985 movie. Whenever I look at that picture it reminds me of those early start-up days when on the wings of a prayer we succeeded against the odds. Every time I see that picture, it gives my confidence a jolt and makes me smile.

With every achievement, large or small, you increase your strength and confidence. It makes me think of the comic book character, the Green Lantern, who was introduced in the 1940s. The Green Lantern possesses a ring that provides the wearer with incredible power and abilities by harnessing willpower. The power depletes over time and the Green Lantern must recharge it by sticking his hand into a lantern for a brief moment and reciting his commitment to protect against evil: "In the brightest day, in the blackest night, no evil shall escape my sight. Let those who worship evil's might, beware my power ... Green Lantern's light!"

The superpower of confidence needs to be recharged with new stories and with the vision of new achievements. Recite your commitment: *I have been successful before, I will be successful again. I am a capable, confident, and able person. I believe in a future where I am succeeding with new opportunities and achievements.* Be specific in your mantra. Include things that you have successfully achieved in the past and the details of the goals you wish to achieve in the immediate or long-term future.

Take out a fresh piece of paper and write down every single positive achievement you can think of. The first time you rode your bike, got a great mark on an assignment you worked hard at, aced a job interview. Think about projects you initiated, executed, and got to the finish line. Have you volunteered or performed a selfless act? Write it all down. Don't hold back; it's just you and a piece of paper. Now take a step back and look at all those things on that list. Wow! You should be feeling stronger and more encouraged already.

Here's your evidence: *You are capable, strong, and powerful; you can move through walls. You have been successful in the past and you will be successful in the future. There are so many more victories to come.* Doesn't that mantra send shivers of excitement through you? It does for me every time I do this exercise. It makes me feel like a superhero who has just landed in the middle of a road that has been cracked by my force, with cars strewn all over, and people running for cover. Muscles bulging, fists clenched in determination, I'm ready: *Let's go!*

One thing I've learned over the course of my business career is that clarity breeds confidence. When I was running Links, I found myself at times dealing with simple issues that would escalate out of control. I realized that my team had started to take the path of least resistance, which represented a lack of confidence. This was creating a "pass the buck" culture where one person's problem got passed along to the next, and to the next; at the end of day, no one really understood the root of the problem or was any closer to solving it. The result was that no one felt they owned the issue and it festered. To address this issue, I developed an acronym for a practice I would call C.R.A.T.E., which stood for clarity, responsibility, accountability, transparency, and excellence. The idea was to empower team members to see themselves as directly connected to the success of the company and to give them the confidence to take ownership and act when problems came their way. To do this, C.R.A.T.E encouraged front-line members to seek complete clarity on anything that would cross their desk and drill down to the root of an issue when it came to their attention.

The system worked. As people acquired more knowledge, they realized they could solve issues and became accountable. This clarity inspired greater confidence, and it had a significant, positive accelerating effect. Each time a team member successfully dealt with a problem, their confidence increased.

The acronym held up: When you start by pursuing clarity, accountability and responsibility follow—in fact, they naturally occur in the course of making clarity a demand in any situation— and the end result is excellence.

Demanding clarity "in the moment" is useful as well. It's easy to just nod our heads in understanding at the many things thrown at us throughout the day. This can happen at work but also at home. We are doing one thing while thinking of something else. What would happen if every time we took action we sought clarity and intent first? Almost everything we do would result in excellence. And excellence breeds greatness.

Confidence starts with actively loving yourself. *You have compassion for others, why not yourself?* Self-compassion is the practice of being aware and accepting that you are not perfect and that you may fail, even after doing your best. Note, however, that just because you failed at a task does not mean you did not succeed. The real failure is not doing everything within your capability to succeed. The most important lessons in life are learned through our journeys.

Extend the same understanding that you would give others and grant yourself permission to go back and try again. W.E. Hickson (1803–1870), a British educator, is credited for popularizing the following phrase:

> *'Tis a lesson you should heed:*
> *Try, try, try again.*
> *If at first you don't succeed,*
> *Try, try, try again.*

Perseverance is its own confidence booster. Not every project we undertake will go smoothly, and sometimes we will have to fail along the way to ultimately achieve success. In the moment, the emotions of not succeeding in the way you expected can be a challenge. Think of this though, it's far easier to not take a risk; the choice to do nothing at all is like never stepping outside your house. When you try something new—even if it doesn't work out as you intended—you've succeeded. Put your best foot forward and continue to love and believe in yourself regardless of the outcome. Be kind to yourself, and if you don't succeed, *try, try, and try again.*

When I had the vision for Cybermind, I was so impassioned that I just kept battling my way forward despite the obstacles in my path. After negotiating a relationship with technology partners in the UK, I set out to get financing. I think I was turned down by every bank. Then, I was turned down by every retail location I approached. But I kept going, and after a while I started to feel like every failure just made me stronger. It confirmed that I believed in my dream more than anything that stood in my way. And I learned something new from each setback, paving the way for my eventual moment of success.

You'll never know failure or success unless you try. You've probably heard the phrase: *If it was easy, everyone would do it!* Being successful requires endurance, perseverance, and tenacity. It also requires taking risks. Many of the world's most successful people, outliers like Steve Jobs and Elon Musk, blew past conventional thinking in pursuit of a powerful vision they knew to be true, and they absolutely encountered obstacles and failures along the way! The difference between them and others is that they persevered. There are no rewards without risk, and no success without the fortitude to keep going when everything is against you. From my personal experience, there is no sweeter feeling—or bigger confidence booster—than taking a risk and succeeding in the dream.

A final note on failure. When we fail, it is sometimes tempting to blame other people or circumstances beyond our control. Try to resist this urge. When we take responsibility for both our successes and failures, we exert control over our life, which increases our personal power and builds our confidence.

You can choose to use your failures as an excuse to stay down or as a reason to succeed. One path will maintain the status quo; the other path will lead you to your greatness.

Canadians are one of the politest people you will ever come across. We are always apologizing for something; the word "sorry" is habitual in our conversations. We are sorry for being first through a door, we are sorry for bumping into each other, we are sorry for being late. Sometimes we aren't sorry for any reason at all; we just say it to open a conversation. To some extent, the word has lost its original intent; we now use it to show our consideration for others, which is "nice." But here's the thing: Using "sorry" reflexively like this can have the effect of inadvertently undermining our confidence.

I was recently listening in on a sales call where one of my employees repeated the word several times during a conversation: "Hello, this is Alex, I'm really sorry if I caught you at a bad time." When someone says they're sorry in this sort of habitual way, it feels as if they are apologizing for their very existence, for being in another's space. Saying sorry like this is a non-confidence vote in yourself, and saying it again and again limits your opportunity for a future with others. By selling yourself short, you are in fact selling your relationship short, and passing along your lack of confidence to others.

Instead of apologizing, rephrase the conversation: *I'm so grateful I have the opportunity to speak with you today.* Saying sorry out of context will inadvertently push people away. Stating your gratitude will always draw people near.

Being a confident person is about putting yourself out there. To take initiative and self-advocate, you need to be willing to go outside of your comfort zone. When you do this, however, people will sometimes label your confidence as arrogance. These accusations can often be a cover-up to mask others' insecurities or envy. It is hurtful to be judged this way, and by taking others' comments personally your confidence can be undermined, thereby achieving the accuser's goal. We all like having the approval of others, but this is not always a healthy impulse. I have often had people tell me why I "couldn't" do something. If I had listened to them, where would I be today? Accusations of arrogance reflect the mindset of the accuser, not yours.

Real arrogance is insecurity masking itself as confidence. It's a con game and is often accompanied by a lack of openness, a strong bias, and heightened narcissism. Arrogant people have no patience for listening to others and are often quick to accuse others of arrogance. Confidence, on the other hand, is not swayed or intimidated by what others think or say; that non-conformity is the basis for creative disruption and achieving greatness. Confident people listen to others and stay grounded by being open to the world around them. Accusations of arrogance are often naturally dispelled with time.

If we present ourselves honestly and follow through with our actions, we can often change people's perceptions of us. And at other times it's just best to ignore them. In a competitive environment, people will use all sorts of accusations to get an advantage, and we need to maintain a thick skin. Instead of becoming defensive, recognize these accusations for what they are and move forward objectively. The more confident you become, the less others' opinions will matter.

Self-examination is always important. If we practice openness, faith, forgiveness, and belief in our future on a daily basis, we will stay humble. This humility will protect us against overconfidence and increase our listening and empathy skillset.

When confidence is not grounded in humility and mindfulness, it can become myopic and hurtful to others. Even when you are not arrogant but have a healthy self-confidence, you need to check your ego and pride at the door to achieve larger goals, especially when your success depends on working with others. I have seen lives and businesses ruined when people cannot rein it in.

This, in fact, happened to a mentor of mine, who showed me profound kindness and support. He was part of a successful family business and a hard worker with high expectations for himself and the people around him. I always thought of him as confident and clear; he lived a magnanimous life. And then one day he must have felt that he was deserving of more. He wanted to lead the company, but his brothers refused him. It was the beginning of the end of a great company, which became mired in family conflict fueled by my mentor's sense of being betrayed.

The company and the family eventually crumpled under the weight of lawsuits and in-fighting. It got so bad, there was just no way out. There was no humility, appreciation, or gratefulness for what they built; all that was left was the ensuing disappointment and injustice each felt. I loved and respected this man dearly, and he left me with a valuable lesson. There have been moments while sitting in a boardroom when I have felt disrespected or offended and experienced the heat rise in my chest—desperate to stand up for myself—but instead I held my tongue and kept my eye on the endgame. The result has usually been money in the bank.

Building your self-confidence speaks to this truth: Every time you put yourself out there, take a risk, and add a new story to your life, you are reinforcing your confidence. I take my inspiration from some amazing people I know.

My good friend Mark is a master at the confidence game. Watching him work with people is like observing an artist in the midst of a creative whirlwind. Mark demands no attention or respect; he doesn't have to. He has an uncanny ability to get people to adopt his ideas and believe in themselves. He is sincere, and he delivers the goods. Over the 30 years that I have known and worked with Mark, he has been one of my greatest fans and has always encouraged me. "How can I help you?" he always asks. Mark and I have done well together because we focus on the endgame, and we typically have one hell of a time getting there!

A few years back I joined Mark and his brother Ron in working on a great project called FoodReach. Mark had followed his purpose and was inspired to create a program to bring healthy food to those in need, through social agencies. Ron's company was going to help with the supply chain and I was to provide the technology. One morning, Ron didn't feel well and checked himself into the hospital. Things went terribly wrong very quickly, and Mark ended up losing his brother and best friend. The thing is, Mark did not miss a beat. He continued to ask everyone what he could do to help them. I know that he hurt for his brother, but instead of letting his loss destroy him it made him even more aware of the gift of every moment in life.

Henry Fleishman lived to be a young and spry 94 years old. He was a Holocaust survivor who was always off on new adventures, and created new stories even in his later life. His love for life was so vivacious, he was an inspiration to all who knew him. One cruise line would give him free passage so that he would dance with single patrons on the ship. Henry liked his Single Malt, and I seriously could not keep up with him. "My *dochtor* told me I shouldn't *dvink* so much," he told me. "Meanwhile he's dead and I'm still drinking." He laughed and took my hand, and with a straight face, he continued: "Life is like this, yesterday is the past, today is reality, and tomorrow is a dream."

I was privileged to attend the 100th birthday party of David Anisman. David was a philanthropist who started an endowment that helps young people study in Israel. He also raised millions of dollars for the Jerusalem College of Technology, which encourages people within the religious community who have little exposure to a secular education to pursue a career towards practical employment. David Anisman's name is synonymous with giving. I was always impressed that he would ask after each one of my children by name and he would remember what they were up to. Every so often I would get a call from David inviting me to his hobby farm just north of Toronto; it was always last minute. "Be here at 3PM," he'd say in his distinctive crackling voice. He always lived in the moment. If I would try to decline, he'd laugh and say, "It's not wise to take a rain check with me."

David had this wonderful property with the most opulent horse stables, and he produced the best fruits and vegetables I have ever tasted. I remember one time I was up there and he had my youngest boys, Dov and Dean, working pitchforks raising potatoes, and I asked him in the midst of the unearthing process, "David, what's your secret?" He gave me an exasperated look and gestured out to the land around him. "What the hell do you think?" he said. "Buy a farm!"

Every time I think of that conversation, it puts a smile on my face, because despite his obvious dismay at my clichéd question, he did indeed provide the answer. What he was saying was to look around and buy into something that allows you to breathe, to grow, and to regenerate. Work your life everyday as you would the earth, and yield from it the rewards of planting the seeds and nurturing growth. Create new stories. This is the final key to confidence: *Live.*

Confidence highlighted:

1. Every action we take is directly related to our confidence.
2. To stay confident in difficult situations, keep your eye on the endgame. Focus on what you "need" to happen rather than what you "want" to happen.
3. Fear is a natural response to things we can't control. Take the mystery out of fear, and it will lose much of its power over you.
4. Clarity breeds confidence.
5. Confidence starts with actively loving yourself.
6. To achieve greatness, check your ego and pride at the door.
7. Increase your confidence by making new positive life stories happen.

Chapter Seven

FIND YOUR PURPOSE

*The way you get meaning into your life is to devote
yourself to loving others, devote yourself to your
community around you, and devote yourself to creating
something that gives you purpose and meaning.*

-*Mitch Albom,* Tuesdays with Morrie

One of my favorite novels is *The Alchemist*, by Paulo Coelho (1988). *The Alchemist* recounts the story of a sheep herder who seeks to follow a dream about a treasure. The idea is that we all have dreams, but how many of us make the commitment to follow them? Coelho calls these dreams "personal legends." I call them one's "life purpose." Whatever term you use, deciding to pursue something that gives your life meaning will start you on a journey where there is an opportunity for things to happen that you could have never imagined.

It was not until I was in my mid-thirties that I started to really understand the role "purpose" played in my life. I hadn't spent much time thinking about my own purpose until I sensed there was a void. Over time, this void seemed to grow and sap away my energy and motivation. As the void deepened, it became wider, and as a result I became more reactive in my life. This reactiveness was a decelerator to my confidence. There was so much going right in my life, yet I felt that something was profoundly missing. I experienced what I would come to recognize as a "crisis of purpose."

A crisis of purpose transcends age, experience, and background. Often, when I ask people about their future, I will get answers of varying ambiguity. Many will admit to feeling a sense of loss for something they can't quite put their finger on. During these conversations, there is often anxiety and uncertainty, the void and the fear laid bare in their eyes. They are also experiencing a crisis in purpose.

So why has purpose become so scarce? What has happened in our society that makes it so difficult to find our purpose, despite having access to more information, opportunities, and "things" than ever before? Perhaps this excess is part of the problem; our busy lives conspire against moments of reflection and deep inquiry into our souls. Every day, we are inundated by information and media. Our society rewards multi-tasking and perpetual engagement. All those avenues of possibility can prove distracting, making it difficult to commit to a single task or direction. With so many choices and frames-per-second stimulation it is no wonder that so many people suffer from ADHD.

As we get older, the pressure to be "connected" only deepens. We live busy, multi-dimensional lives, dividing our attention between our jobs, families, hobbies, online activities, chores, and friendships. It can be absolutely overwhelming. *Where do we fit in the time to think about what we value, and what we want to be?* No wonder we struggle to find balance between keeping up and moving forward with purpose!

> *I find myself doing one thing and thinking about five other things, to the point that I lose track of the moment I am experiencing.*

So what is purpose? Purpose is something we passionately believe in and serve through the way we live our lives; when we act in accordance with our purpose, we receive our greatest feelings of accomplishment. For some, their purpose is apparent from a young age; for others, their purpose can remain dormant for much of their lives, or may never be realized.

Studies have shown that people with purpose live longer. As a part of a study reported in *Lancet*, a medical science journal, about 9,000 people over the age of 65 were surveyed over an 8.5-year period. They were given a questionnaire that gauged how much control they felt they had over their lives and how much they thought what they did was worthwhile. The participants were then split into four groups, ranging from the highest to the lowest levels of well-being. Over the course of the study, 9% of people in the highest well-being category died compared to 29% in the lowest category. Clearly, feeling a sense of purpose has some profound implications for the quality of our lives, although many of us struggle at times to define it.

Do you know what gives you a sense of purpose? Can you articulate it? These are important questions to answer. When we consider purpose at a conscious level, we become more mindful of the life we are living and can better understand what we want from our lives in the future.

I was driving with my son and his 13-year-old friend one afternoon, and making small talk. "Aaron, what does your dad do?" I asked my son's friend. "Oh, he's an accountant," Aaron replied. "And what do you want to do?" I asked. "I'm not really sure, but whatever it is I want to be happy and enjoy it," was his answer. I was blown away by the simplicity of his response and how naturally it rolled off his tongue. At thirteen, this kid had just stated his core purpose.

Discovering purpose requires an examination of our core values. Core values are the fundamental personal beliefs that often dictate our behavior and actions. These values shape our lives. In fact, many of the communities we are part of form as a result of shared values. For example, in our relationship, my wife and I share values that shape many of our practical decisions, such as which schools our children attend, what synagogue we belong to, and how we treat the Sabbath, etc.

Core values are integral to our relationships. When someone in a relationship changes their belief in the value system that underpins the original foundation of the relationship, it can threaten the bonds formed. This change might be positive for the person making it, but if it affects others, it must happen slowly, with consent and sensitivity, if the relationship is to survive.

I experienced this situation when my parents underwent a religious awakening. I was not on board, so I was out. Being alienated like that affected how I felt about myself for a long time.

When we make a major shift in life, it is important to consider how it might affect others. The human psyche does not respond well when forced to adhere to an extreme shift in values. Each person deserves to have their needs considered with empathy, patience, and unconditional acceptance. Relationships are strengthened by a willingness to compromise, take things slowly, and find a new norm. This consideration empowers everyone in a relationship to make their own choices, which strengthens love and commitment. And when people feel they have a choice, they are more likely to make objective, measured, and accepting decisions.[5]

One of my core values in my business practice is accountability. When something happens, I expect my team to take responsibility and act to remedy the situation. The truth will always make itself known; the only thing to do is to get out in front of it. I ask them to show respect and to recognize the situation for what it is. Fixing it may not be pretty, but I believe we will achieve more if the relationship survives. To achieve this, we have to be upfront and transparent, and act with integrity. Even if we cannot save the relationship, I can live with it if we have done our best to address the situation and are accountable for what happened. This is an example of how a core value trickles down into action.

Here is an exercise. On an empty sheet of paper, write a list of your values. Everything from religion to your taste in music. Identify the values that have a clearly defined goal. These are your "core values."

---

[5] This consideration is especially true for children. Don't underestimate how decisions affect children. By asking their opinions and involving them in the process of change, you can achieve far greater buy-in, smoothing the process and minimizing collateral damage. Children don't want to feel forgotten during the process of change; after all, your changes affect their lives too.

This exercise may bring forward values and goals that you have not paid attention to. The effect of writing everything down is that these values will become more real.

Now, list the core values of people you have relationships with, as well as the core values associated with your career. Observe the alignments. The more parallels, the greater the chance you will feel fulfilled in the relationship. Fewer parallels between value systems may explain why a relationship or career leaves you feeling drained. Finding people and career options that share your core values will create healthier connections and a healthier you.

In his book *Outliers: The Story of Success* (2008), Malcolm Gladwell posits that there is a class of people he calls "outliers" who are differentiated by their passion and commitment to their vocation. He defines them as people who have spent over 10,000 hours in the pursuit of excellence in their field. While most of these people were born with a talent or skillset, it is their passion that drives them and sets them apart. He cites examples like the Beatles, Steve Jobs, Oprah Winfrey, and Bill Gates, people with very different focuses who nevertheless share a level of commitment that led them to become the best at what they do.

There are many other notable people who fit this criterion and have dedicated their lives to altruistic causes. For Mother Theresa, it was feeding the poor. For Gandhi, Martin Luther King, and Rabbi Abraham Joshua Heschel, it was the fight for human equality.

This passion and dedication, along with a commitment to excellence, is what living with purpose looks like. We may not all get to be, or want to be, billionaires or media moguls or living saints, but we all have the same number of hours in a day, the same number of days in a year, and we get to choose how we spend them. This is the simple secret outliers have discovered.

Many of us will find our purposes evolve over the course of our lives; this is part of the journey. We can commit to actions that achieve ends that are greater than ourselves. We can override our comfort zones, shrug off other people's expectations, and surpass our material wants to get to a sustained engagement with our purpose.

I once met someone who had spent years studying to become a neurosurgeon, and yet only a couple of years into practicing, he decided he was going to quit medicine to write science fiction. It was a decision many people close to him questioned, but he was not deterred. From his perspective, he had spent years doing what others had expected of him, but the personal cost was too high.

I'm not saying that purely dedicating ourselves to our passions is always practical, but this story speaks to a truth about purpose: The more we dedicate ourselves to something we are not passionate about, the further we move away from feeling purposeful. Inversely, doing what we are passionate about will always result in feeling purposeful in our life. To find our passion, we must listen to ourselves and be aware. Pursuing a purpose is an act of self-confidence and will open the gateway to your personal greatness.

After the death of my mother, Toby Kippen, one of my mother's closest and oldest friends, threw me a life vest and brought me to California to spend the summer with her family. The experience left an indelible impression on me; I saw in them an example of people who lived their lives on their own terms, and it made me aware that this was possible.

Toby met her husband and love of her life, Ian, while finishing a PhD in microbiology at UCLA. Midlife, while living in the Palisades, Toby became a dentist and Ian a noted jazz musician. They moved to Israel for three years to give their son the experience of living in the Holy Land, then they moved to Atlanta to be with their daughters; there, Toby studied to become a Hebrew language teacher. In retirement, they reinvented themselves as real estate entrepreneurs. When Ian suddenly died, Toby was devastated, but it didn't stop her from continuing to pursue her passions. At 75 years of age, she completed an advanced Hebrew language degree at Hebrew University.

Toby exemplifies the pursuit of passion to create meaning and purpose in her life. In all her vocations, she achieved her personal greatness and was well-respected by her peers and colleagues. As her reality evolved, so did her purpose; she made choices to follow her passion. She did this while having amazing relationships, inspiring others, and raising a family. Toby's life trajectory shows that there is no rule that says you are restricted to one career or one passion. Similarly, I look at career moves and business opportunities as events in my life that have taken me to where I am meant to be. It's all part of this wonderful journey.

Commitment, perseverance, strategy, hard work, and a good deal of luck can be key factors to success; openness and faith remove barriers, enabling us to listen and perceive in acute ways. Belief in a future and self-confidence are other essentials. But purpose is the rocket fuel that will project you into a new realm. The life of an entrepreneur can often be isolating. Until you achieve success or look like you might, positive feedback can be brief and scarce. Having purpose is what keeps us moving forward; it introduces structure and discipline into the uncertainty and helps us trust that we will reach the finish line.

We all have a purpose. It's a matter of observing the world around you and "feeling" what fits. Job shadowing is an excellent process to help a young person start to think about what path or livelihood may impart a sense of purpose. A healthy mind, body, and soul will help you tap into your strongest intuitive self. When you find your purpose, there will be a sort of heat in your core telling you that you've arrived. You will know you're there.

Simon Sinek is one of my favorite contemporary authors and speakers. I was fortunate to hear him as the keynote speaker at a conference I attended. He talked about the "just cause." As Sinek defines it, the just cause is "more than your 'why' or purpose, a just cause is what motivates you to get out of bed in the morning. It's the passion or hunger that burns inside that compels you to do what you do. Your just cause is what powers you to outlast your competitors. It propels you forward in the face of adversity and empowers you to persevere when you feel like giving up."

Each of us has something deeply rooted within that will defy reason and norms, that will help us push past barriers in our path. To achieve greatness, we must tap into this latent power.

What I love and find meaning in is starting up and running businesses. It doesn't matter to me particularly what industry I'm in because what I'm passionate about is the process of enterprise building; this is one of my purposes. What did I know about virtual reality technology, warehousing, software development, hospitality, when I started these businesses? I knew they were good business opportunities, and I trusted my intuition and experience to help me with the rest.

Every time I start a business, I feel an incredible sense of optimism and excitement; every day I wake up to great possibilities and unknowns. I love it, all the nuances, even the bad days when I have to right the ship to see the results of my vision unfold. And I'm good at it. I know about investments, structuring, operations, risk assessments, marketing, sales, and performance.

Running a business I visualize myself as a captain guiding his ship with a steady hand in times of turbulent waters. Seeing my vision unfold is like an act of creation. This is what I've become an outlier in.

But my sense of professional purpose is also evolving. In fact, that's why this book exists. Over the years, I've come to realize that helping people find purpose and meaning in their own lives gives me purpose. I enjoy the *a-ha* moment when people realize their own solutions to their problems through our conversations. In turn, listening to others and observing their actions has taught me a great deal about myself and helped me to develop the philosophy espoused in this book, and the practices that ground it. This book is a gateway to fulfilling that higher purpose.

What are you doing in your life to help you uncover your purpose? Your purpose is fundamental to who you are, what you value, and what drives you. Your purpose acts as an inner guide and creates a connection between your actions and sense of self. In other words, you are what you do and what you do affects how you feel about yourself. What makes purpose so hard to define is that even as it informs our actions, it is being informed by our actions. Our purpose is somewhat circular and continues to reveal itself as we act on it. These actions occur on so many different levels that purpose comes to affect every part of our lives: our relationships, health, happiness, and spirituality. And we may have more than one purpose. In fact, many of us have a hierarchy of purposes.

Let's take a pause here and ask ourselves this question. *Are you cognizant of your hierarchy of purposes?* Start with one thing that you think acts as a purpose in your life. Say it out loud. As your lips form these words, consider their validity and how they make you feel. If it sounds right and feels good, chances are what you just verbalized belongs in your hierarchy. Now articulate another purpose in your life. Keep going until you have a list.

Don't worry if it feels like some things on your list are bigger or more important than others. Some of our purposes will be greater than others; some will develop to become more important, and some will remain life-long pursuits while the importance of others will fade away. This is a natural process that coincides with what stage we are in life. The important thing here is to feel the power behind the words. It is freeing and empowering to recognize you have a purpose, and to be able to articulate what your purpose actually is. Knowing your purposes will alleviate anxieties or confirm something you may have long felt but could not articulate.

If you are struggling to discover your purposes, take a step back and consider these questions. *What have you achieved that has left you with a strong sense of fulfillment? What are you good at? What would you die for? What do you live for? What do you do that makes you lose track of time?* Think of your experiences, then find the commonalities and connect the dots. Follow the breadcrumbs and you will find your hierarchy of purpose.

Our hierarchy of purpose changes as we enter different stages in life and as we become more mindful. It makes sense that as we mature and our life situation changes so do our priorities. Sometimes, it can be certain events that happen in our lives that light that fire.

I was 20 years old and in the south of Spain. Traveling alone, I was hitchhiking along a road trying to get to Madrid. It was dusk and I had just been let out of a ride. Once the dust from the tires settled and the car was a distant speck, I found some cover near the road in a natural shelter carved from some boulders, similar to the mouth of a shallow cave. As I settled in to wait out the night, I started to feel very alone. I was gripped by a sudden anxiety that I could be robbed and murdered in this place. Buried right there at the side of the road. No one would know where I was, who I was, or where I had been. The anxiety I felt in that moment made me think that my life could end at any moment and if it did, it would have meant nothing. It was a very scary thought.

Without warning, I started to heave out years of tears and over the course of that long, lonely night, I re-evaluated my life. One thought came to my mind with a jolt. I had to go to school and get an education. It was that simple. I had dropped out of high school in tenth grade, but now the truth hit me. If I wanted my life to mean something, I would need to learn to speak the language and understand the world I lived in. As soon as I returned home, I enrolled in university. In that moment, my priorities shifted, and my purpose evolved.

Shortly after my daughter was born, she came down with a fever, a serious symptom in a newborn. I remember the terror I felt. My back supported by the wall behind me, I slid down to a seated position on the floor in the emergency room. On the other side of the room the doctor on call was conducting a spinal tap on my little girl. Her cries sent shivers down my spine. In that moment, I realized her life meant more to me than my own. It was the first time that my life felt truly less important than someone else's. Another shift.

I'll never forget the time my eldest son, Eitan, crawled into bed with us one evening. He was in his final year of high school and terribly anxious about not knowing what to do when he graduated. I was moved seeing the tears streaming down his cheeks. He was scared that he had no purpose or direction. It turned out to be a defining moment in his life. A couple of weeks later he came to us and informed us of his intentions to join the Israeli army. I questioned his sincerity and if he understood the gravity of this commitment. Over the next several months, however, seeing his conviction and careful preparation, I was convinced that this was a real purposeful commitment for him.

Looking back, I am so proud that he pursued his purpose; his experiences have allowed him to understand himself and explore the world in a way that he would not have done at home. The thought of spending his first year at university, pub-hopping with his buddies, did not fit with his hierarchy of purpose. He made a choice to strike out in a different direction. It illustrated his deep desire to live his life purposefully. When Limore and I stood under the hot July sun at Eitan's graduation ceremony, where he was presented with the Soldier of Excellence award, it was one of our proudest moments as parents.

⌒

Purposes fall within two categories: eudemonic (finding purpose in serving others) and hedonomic (finding purpose in serving ourselves). People driven by eudemonic purposes believe what they do affects the world and circles back to them. People driven by hedonomic purposes chase their own consumption and pleasures; they only believe in furthering their own success. While these definitions suggest we should all want to be driven by eudemonic purposes, the reality is that most of us will have a mixture of purposes, and some will fall into both categories. For example, running a business is, by nature, self-serving. We can, however, make choices for our business that are in service of others, like treating our employees well or using the firm's resources to contribute to charity.

The philosopher John Jacques Rousseau (France; 1712–1778) argued that man is exclusively and ultimately self-serving because we act within a societal system that has corrupted our natural goodness. One could also argue that that there are rewards for acting according to eudemonic purposes, which is in itself self-serving. The reality is that almost all of us have eudemonic purposes because these relate to our relationships with others and the world; they are the way we try to make the world a better place.

It is well-documented that people who base their actions on eudemonic purposes live longer and stay healthier than those who live their lives hedonistically. For example, a research study of 500 persons between the ages of 70 and 103 over a 20-year period found that grandparents who looked after their grandchildren had a 34% lower mortality rate.[6] In another study, mortality rates were 22% lower for people who volunteered their time.[7] In the same study it was discovered that volunteers experience less depression and more meaning in their lives. Living your life with an emphasis on eudemonic purposes will add years to your life and help you live happier.

I made a conscious choice early in life to put faith on my hierarchy of purpose. To do that, I had to separate the religion I belonged to from the people who tried to use it to hurt and control me. I intuitively came to the conclusion that you can't judge Judaism by the Jew … nor Christianity by the Christian, nor Islam by the Muslim. I chose to continue to love and respect my faith, and to not define it or judge it by the actions of a few individuals.

The truth is, I love my Judaism. I have found peace within a balanced observance of its rituals. My wife and I made a conscious choice that we wanted to raise our children to "celebrate" their Jewish roots as a primary purpose in their lives. "Man-made" interpretations and practices can sometimes be a way to control others. Don't

---

[6] Published in the journal *Evolution and Human Behavior* (2016)

[7] Published in *BMC Public Health* (2013)

allow people to take away something that gives you joy and purpose.

Knowing your purpose is a grounding force. It may be the observance of a religious or cultural practice; it may come from an appreciation of art or science; it may come from community work. Your purpose may be found in a place that brings you peace. Whatever it is that grounds you, it is important to honor that purpose in your life and way of life.

I was thinking about this concept while watching Sandra Bullock in the film *Gravity* (2013). Imagine you, like Sandra, are floating in space. There is nothing connecting you, nothing holding you back; this is perfect freedom. But you are also in danger of slowly spinning out of control in that vast universe. Now imagine you have a tether, and with that tether you can pull yourself back to the mothership, a place where you can regain your footing, so to speak. Purpose is that tether. It can bring you home when you are lost. It can connect you to the people and places that are the most important to you. When I became a father, I realized how important it was to provide that tether to my children. Each generation breathes a newness into the world and with that a need to find their sense of purpose and place.

In Victor Strecher's book *Life on Purpose* (2016), he writes about a conversation he had with an acquaintance from Uganda. James became an orphan at the age of 10, when both his parents died of AIDs. He was raised by his grandmother, and against vast odds, he went on to receive a master's degree in public health.

I don't think anyone could have blamed James if he had just got by in life, but he was motivated by intuition, a calling, and a passion to help people, which pushed him to achieve far more than many people who grew up in better circumstances. Strecher quotes James as saying he has two passions in life. His first was to leave behind a better world, "where everyone who has been denied opportunity can achieve their dreams and vision in life." The second was to make each individual interaction count, so the people he met left feeling better than when they arrived. "Families that break down," James told Strecher, "are the ones who have no purpose or vision for the family. Purpose goes hand and hand with hope. Hope for their children. Hope for a better life. In the West, people may not relate to this, but this is how we think. Purpose sustains poor people."

With that statement, James accesses the bigger picture of why it is so important to find your purpose in life, and to then let it give guidance to the way you live and act. Purpose has the power to change not just your life, but the world. Being purposeful is about taking a position. It requires you to draw a line in the sand and make a commitment to something. You have to proclaim: *This is who I am.* Knowing your purpose requires you to know and honor yourself and the world around you. Can you imagine if we all lived with the attitude of James?

Ironically, in an age where we have the greatest choice and most freedoms, many people suffer from a crisis of purpose. Purpose is derailed by the obliviousness of ourselves and others, by a constant striving for instant gratification, by self-serving consumption, and even by the very ease of our lives.

In the first chapter of this book, I discussed my deep concerns about the alarming increase in deaths by overdose.

Young people, especially, seem to be falling victim to the epidemic of powerful synthetic drugs that mercilessly snuff out their promising lives. There are no boundaries to this crisis; it has affected all levels of society, all genders, races, and classes. I do not believe that many of the victims intended their own demise.

Which leads me to ask: *Why do these young people feel the need to augment their lives in this way, especially when the consequences can be fatal? Why, with all the publicity and awareness, do they risk everything for a few hours of euphoria without regard to the consequences?*

The only answer I can come up with is that they must be experiencing intense boredom, one that has robbed them of their senses and caused them to lose not just their sense of purpose but their big-picture meaning of life.

Why don't they have enough stimulation in their lives? A generation of young people are spiraling out of control without any tethering to bring them back.

Let me present you with a theory. I believe this situation is happening because the very idea of a larger purpose has become an abstraction. This crisis is borne not out of deprivation, but overabundance. My generation of parents, having grown up in perhaps too controlled of an environment, have adopted a more liberal attitude towards our children; but as a result, we sometimes struggle to set appropriate boundaries and instill appropriate values in our children.

As parents, we can be afraid of rocking the boat. We subsequently give far too much rope to our kids, enough rope to hang themselves—in some cases literally! I believe the answer is that we have to set boundaries, but with consensus.

"Setting boundaries by consensus" may, however, sound like an oxymoron. Boundaries and consensus seem to be at opposite ends of the spectrum. Though it is important to be firm about the boundaries we set, we also need to explain our rationalization and seek consensus. This is where the boundaries and consensus may intersect and align. This discussion allows children to feel like they are a part of the process and fosters agreement through consensus, while teaching them to deal with not getting their way all the time.

It is important to draw a line and stick to it, even if we want to give our children everything under the sun. If I am not comfortable with the "chill" arrangements that my 14 year old is selling me on, then it's up to me to set boundaries. By bringing our children into the decision-making process, we teach them to do the same. Purpose thrives when a person is empowered, and it is never too early to start the journey.

We live in a society where it is very easy to lose ourselves. The competition to come first is intense. Take Miami traffic. People will risk their own and everyone else's lives to buy an additional few seconds of time by weaving in and out of traffic on the I-95 at high speeds. Collectively, the culture has developed such an aggressive driving behavior because no one gives anyone else an inch, though the results can be deadly.

Observing how people behave in traffic can be very telling. I remember waiting in traffic at a 4-way light in Tel Aviv. Every time a vehicle freed up some space, everyone would move forward at the same time, creating gridlock. Aggressive driving behavior is self-centered, and it often ends up taking you longer to get where you want to go!

In the long run, living a purposeful life favors living with empathy and consideration. Increases in urban density will naturally place people in a position to fight for their survival, *OMG! I need my non-fat, dairy-free grande latte right now! And can you believe how slow this line is?!* This self-centered intensity does not best serve our common humanity.

Serving a single good—ourselves—is finite; serving the common good is infinite. When we feel imbalanced, it is often a sign that we have lost track of what truly gives us purpose. To address this issue, we must adjust and reconnect with our hierarchy of purpose. Spend two minutes and ask yourself: *How do I feel about who I am as a person? Am I being true to my purpose?*

One day, an employee I had spent much time coaching and had high hopes for walked into my office and quit. I did not see it coming. He explained that he felt he was not getting anywhere. He did not have other plans; he just didn't feel a sense of purpose. Even though I did not agree with him, I had to respect the guy for putting his sense of purpose above drawing a salary. It's not often you come across that kind of principled stand. He may not have made what I thought was a smart move, but he did remain true to himself. When you do that, the choices you make will always energize you. Those decisions will unlock your future and feed the purpose that drives you, leading you to the meaningful existence you seek.

When I compromise myself, it's a strong hit to my self-respect and it devalues me. The reality is, there are times when we make the wrong decisions, give in to something, or pursue immediate gratification. These compromises can crush your momentum. The antidote is to quickly identify and become conscious of the pain-pleasure pattern. By taking responsibility for your actions, you can do something that will restore your balance and put you back into your confidence zone.

Being in the present releases the anxiety of being too wrapped up in the past, and clears the mind to think more about the details of your future. It's easy to go into crisis mode if you feel a sense of "loss" or "emptiness" from not knowing your purpose. At these times, it's important to be aware of and to take a moment to find the calmness of your center. Once there, you can best serve yourself and others.

Remember the hypnagogic state we talked about in Chapter Six? The next time you wake up and find yourself in this relaxed state between consciousness and unconsciousness, try this out—don't rush to get out of bed, stay relaxed, just be there for the moment; breathe deeply and acknowledge yourself. This is the most creative part of your day; listen to the answers that surface.

I will often awake with the answer to something that has been on my mind; it will have the vividness of a dream, and before it retreats back into the recesses of my subconscious, I do my best to relax and capture what I can in order to make sense of the message.

Various practices of meditation can be used to reinforce and focus our purpose, but sitting and thinking about purpose is not enough. Purpose reveals itself through actions. The legendary actress Lucille Ball is credited with the quote: "If you want something done, ask a busy person to do it. The more things you do, the more you can do." Leadership often delegates to people with a strong sense of purpose because these people embody the openness, knowledge, and initiative to put plans into action. That is how ladders are climbed and success is built.

Work environments also foster a sense of purpose. For a very short time, I had what seemed to be a dream corporate job, one that came complete with valet parking, an executive gym membership, and great pay. I would take the GO train some mornings and observe the same people making their way downtown. After a while, I started to feel like I was part of the scene in Alan Parker's trippy movie *Pink Floyd – The Wall* (1982), where the schoolchildren, dressed in identical uniforms, are fed into a meat grinder. While observing the people on the train, I would hum the tune under my breath. I did not find myself useful and it started to eat at me. I ultimately recognized that my need for purpose outweighed the money I was making, and I actually asked to be let out of my contract early. Challenging yourself helps you learn and grow, but a lack of purpose will catch up to you fast.

Purpose is its own renewable energy resource. People with a strong sense of purpose get things done! Purpose produces the motivation to act and bolsters willpower in the face of adversity. Align yourself with others who have a well-defined sense of purpose. When things go wrong, and they will, people with purpose demonstrate more resilience than people without. Purpose instills a commitment to mindful living, which in turn powers the instincts we use to make choices that will help us avoid minefields along the path to our personal greatness.

Earlier in this chapter, I discussed some practical ideas for finding your purpose and suggested mapping out what you think is your purpose, reading it back, and seeing how it makes you feel. Purpose is a knowing feeling. It is meaning brought into your life that transcends the material, the ego, and the subjective. Once you put your mind to finding your purpose, you will become more in tune to doing so. Have faith that your purpose will follow you. It's always been there; you just need to know to look for it. It wasn't until I started writing a book about myself that I began to realize that my true purpose was writing a book for the benefit of others.

Here is an inescapable reality. Life is not always going to be smooth sailing. It likes to remind us how fragile and fleeting this all is. Sometimes, we may feel powerless. However, we have a choice in how we deal with that which makes us feel out of control. At a moment's notice, random events can affect our lives—with devastating effects. Natural disasters, war, illness, death. When this happens, it is our resilience that sees us through, resilience borne of purpose.

In *Man's Search for Meaning* (1946), Frankl describes a "will to meaning." When he was imprisoned in a concentration camp, he told his fellow inmates that there was only one way to survive the horrors, and that was to seek meaning and purpose in order to form the resolve to survive. Frankl said we have a choice: to be victims or victors. Even when we are at our most disenfranchised, having purpose in our lives will build up reserves of resolve—which will be there when we most need it.

Purpose highlighted:

1. A crisis of purpose transcends age, experience, and background.
2. When we act in accordance with our purpose, we receive our greatest feelings of accomplishment.
3. When we consider purpose at a conscious level, we become more mindful of the life we are living, and can better understand what we want from our lives in the future.
4. Discovering purpose requires an examination of core values. Core values are the fundamental personal beliefs that dictate our behavior and actions.
5. You are what you do, and what you do affects how you feel about yourself.
6. Set boundaries by consensus. Give people the control they need over their own lives so they can agree to the boundaries that are set.
7. Living with purpose offsets the risk of boredom.

Chapter Eight

ACCELERATE

People are capable, at any time in their lives, of doing what they dream of.

-*Paulo Coelho*, The Alchemist

It's a beautiful summer morning on the ocean, and the perfect wave is coming in. You've spotted the wave, paddled hard to be in the right position to catch it, and now you are on the top—on the crest. You lean in, commit yourself, and tip the board forward. You invite the surging force of the breaking water to take over, and the result is a massive jolt of acceleration. Looking back, it seems as if everything that happened was pre-destined, there is such perfect harmony between yourself, your purpose, and nature. In that moment, riding atop the surge, is *acceleration.*

> *I have trust in my intuition, powered by the confidence that comes from past achievements. I have done it before; I can do it again.*

Accelerators are positive achievements that propel you forward and reaffirm the faith you have in yourself, which in turns fuels your confidence and leads to even bigger and better things. These can be small projects or significant endeavors that can culminate over years; they can be work-related or come from the fulfillment of a personal goal. Some accelerators result in financial rewards and others in personal fulfillment. What matters is that you commit to them and see them through. By getting to the finish line, no matter what place you finish, you spur your creativity, generate momentum, and build faith in yourself.

Growing up, I never felt particularly smarter than the next person. In fact, in school, it often took me longer to learn things than most of the kids sitting next to me. I struggled with concentration—my brain went a million miles an hour. It still does. With time, however, what I learned was the power to harness ideas and commit to a focus.

It's human nature to want to take the path of least resistance, and if we are not challenged, we won't invent. People who struggle with the "need to achieve" tend not to accept the status quo because they don't function well within it. My life circumstances caused me to become inventive. In his book *Originals* (2016), Adam Grant talks about how some of the most successful people are ordinary people driven to act on their ideas. Grant writes:

> Ultimately, the people who choose to champion originality are the ones who propel us forward. After spending years studying them and interacting with them, I am struck that their inner experiences are not any different from our own. They feel the same fear, the same doubt, as the rest of us. What sets them apart is that they take action anyway. They know in their hearts that failing would yield less regret than failing to try.

There are three stages to the evolution of an idea from first thought to follow through: curiosity, consciousness, and commitment.

Curiosity deals with asking important questions about viability. *Is the opportunity interesting to me? Is this something I should pursue? Does this idea fit into my hierarchy of purpose?* If I get past these questions with positive answers, I have identified something that potentially has some legs to it. I am now curious enough to start the process of disproving the idea.

We are naturally wired to only listen to the answers we "want" to hear, and can easily miss the signs that—on closer inspection—are deal breakers. In the consciousness stage, we take a step back and open ourselves to limitless possibilities. We strip out our biases to see the idea as objectively as possible.

The last question you have to ask yourself is: *Are you prepared to do what it takes?* Money and time are your biggest risk variables. The commitment stage is where decisive action is taken to move an idea forward. With commitment comes passion and purpose. These are fundamental factors, because when the barriers to market test your resolve, it's the overriding sense of purpose and passion that will fuel the ambition and tenacity you will need to push through to the finish line.

To illustrate the evolution of an idea in action, let's return to the example of the virtual reality company I founded. The idea for Cybermind came in a flash. I walked in on the last 10 seconds of *60 Minutes* and Dan Rather was doing a special on this futuristic technology called VR. I immediately had a vision; I saw everything—the business plan, the layout, the opening day—all in six dimensions and in technicolor. Needless to say, my curiosity was piqued.

That was Tuesday; by Thursday morning, I was on a flight to the UK to meet the guys being interviewed. I was driven by something so strong that I became super-focused on this idea.

I fulfilled the curiosity stage: I was interested, and after my initial research, I had a good sense that pursuing this would fit my hierarchy of purpose and was attainable.

In the consciousness stage, I had to remove my biases and be open to what I was seeing. That involved sharing the idea with people, learning more about the technology, and understanding the business opportunity.

One of the key biases I had to get over was my doubt about whether the public would pay for this experience. I was not one to spend money on experiences, and the business counted on people forking over five dollars per game.

The commitment stage involved the actionable items I needed to do to move things forward: the hours spent writing a business plan, knocking on doors, selling my idea. The reality is that curiosity, consciousness, and commitment are not steps that are taken one after another; they act in tandem, and to achieve success, we should constantly be cycling through them.

We should forever be curious and seek out new information. It is important to remain open-minded and not become distracted by our subjective thought process. Consider the facts, talk to the market, ask questions, and trust the data. Finally, we should continuously restate our commitment through our actions.

Cybermind was my vision, and few saw what I did. Doors were slammed in my face. Most people tried to dissuade me. In moments like these, commitment is what keeps us from giving up. Curiosity, consciousness, and commitment are the infrastructure necessary to move any idea forward. This is how we translate a vision into reality.

Curiosity, consciousness, and commitment are especially important as time becomes more scarce and your responsibilities grow. The bigger the idea, the more capital you may need to risk. The need to prioritize and be stingy about what opportunities you pursue becomes necessary in order to safeguard your ability to reach the finish line. I call this filtering the "economics of opportunity."

As a highly creative individual, it's very easy to get caught in the trap of having too many things on the go at the same time. A typical malady of the entrepreneur! It is easy to become overwhelmed. There are only so many hours in a day. Being engulfed in a deluge of ideas and not getting things you commit to to the finish line can ultimately be a significant blow to your confidence.

Without mastering focus, there is a tendency to repeat this cycle over and over again. I know the conundrum well. On the one hand, I have this built-in need to create and accomplish, and on the other hand I need to honor my commitment to the work that needs to get done.

My approach to fleshing out the ideas that I come up with has become more disciplined over time, and with age. To save time, I conduct my due diligence using a process of elimination. I can disprove an idea (or determine it isn't going to work) far faster than I can prove it (or determine it is going to work). Once I am through trying to disqualify my vision, I can then move forward with it, knowing that I have picked something that I have a good chance to succeed at.

Taking an idea from the conception stage to the realization stage is the most powerful type of accelerator I know. Making a commitment is about stepping outside of your comfort zone, and that takes a lot of *chutzpa*! You'll need every bit of confidence you possess to overcome any external and internal doubts.

Commitment requires the discipline to focus on the actions needed to succeed, and to be realistic about what might get in your way. This includes the delegation of tasks to people you need to depend on to get things done. There are some people who are forever scattered and only distract you from the finish line. This is especially true in the creative world! I quickly learned to identify talented people who never learned discipline, something a formal education in most fields will provide. When it comes time to deliver on a commitment, you and your team need the strength to stay on task, avoid all distractions, and keep your eye on the endgame.

This is where the road to good intentions gets bumpy. While it's great to make commitments, you need to achieve milestones to accelerate. If you find yourself long on the talk and short on the walk, you will experience deceleration. Beware of making commitments that you cannot get to the finish line—enough loose threads and your inner confidence and others' faith in you will slowly unravel. Pursue commitments with a firm end date. Create deadlines with a roadmap for every project. And apply all the practices that fuel your best you.

As fear serves to undermine your confidence, procrastination serves to undermine your productivity. I rapidly learned during my early university days to immediately start work on assignments when they were announced, rather than wait until days before they were due. *What you can achieve today needn't be pushed off to tomorrow!*

Procrastinators demonstrate a subconscious desire to suffer the last-minute stress that results from the pressure of looming deadlines. The results are rarely optimal. Your energy is spent reactively, which negatively affects your creativity because you do not have the time to step back and look at the big picture as part of that process. "But I work well under pressure!" many say. For most people, that statement is illusory.

If you are a procrastinator, you need to take responsibility for putting things off. Consciously accept that you receive some form of pleasure from the last-minute pain you go through. Remind yourself at each deadline that your scrambling is actually by design and no one's fault but your own. Often, when we procrastinate, we are building in excuses for failure, in advance.

Become mindful of your accountability in this process and you will be surprised at how quickly you go from procrastinator to planner. Passing the expiration date of a commitment without having given it your all is a definite decelerator and depreciates your potential, morale, and faith in yourself. In contrast, being a planner allows you to adopt a proactive, positive approach, which will accelerate your potential.

Successful entrepreneurs are triumphant because we are big on imposing deadlines right out of the gate and sticking to a checklist of actions and milestones achieved. Giving yourself the best opportunity to succeed is like being able to look down that runway as far as the eye can see, and then visualizing the future ahead. When you do this, you create a positive momentum that comes from being productive and seeing each successive idea through to the next; an amazing benefit is that new ideas surface along the way that only enhance the outcome! Sometimes, however, you can end up in an entirely different place than where you first intended. Make sure the finish line is always in your line of sight, and be relentless about getting there.

When we were at York, my friend Eli Brown and I would regularly take over one of the music rooms and jam together. I would write the lyrics and melody, and Eli would do the musical compilations. I really enjoyed this time we spent together. I would tell Eli that one day when I had the money we would go into a studio and record. I never forgot this commitment. Years later, I called Eli up to see if he wanted to produce some music. We found this great boutique studio with all the bells and whistles.

Over the next few months, we committed to getting this project done. We eventually produced four songs, each of a different genre. I loved the time we spent together, totally dedicated to completing what we set out to do. Five-year old Eitan would come to our sessions, smiling through the soundproof glass as I belted out the vocals. The *Ellis & Brown* CD was completed!

Bringing this personal project to the finish line was a great personal accelerator. Whenever I need a little pick-me-up, I listen to the music we created and am encouraged and strengthened by it, knowing that there is nothing I cannot create and achieve if I put my mind to it. It's an amazing confidence booster!

The message here is to surround yourself with reminders of your accomplishments. These are the accelerators in your life that reaffirm your abilities and remind you that new stories can be made.

I randomly met this guy at my health club. We were in the hot tub, soaking in all our honesty and lost in our individual thoughts. We got to talking as people do.

"So, what do you do?" I asked.

"I practice law," he said.

"Oh, so how's that going?"

"Well you know," he said.

"No," I replied, "I really don't, do tell."

I think he was expecting some blah-blah, generic response, so I may have thrown him for a loop. He paused and then opened up. "You really want to know the truth?" he started. "If I could go back, I would have done something different." He gave a sigh of deep regret. "I really hate it."

"How long have you been doing this for?" I asked.

"Over 30 years now," he responded. The sudden quiet became heavy between us.

I looked up. "So, change it."

He looked at me with these regretful eyes, his speech was controlled. "I can't," he countered.

"Why?" I asked, pushing him to give a deeper answer. He shrugged his shoulders, and I continued to look at him—waiting.

"I have responsibilities, I can't just leave this, I am terrible at this, and I have zero confidence in myself."

I was totally taken aback by his response. "You can't be bad at what you do or be totally without confidence, you've been doing this for so long," I argued.

He continued, "I'm 60 years old, what am I supposed to do now?" Silence again.

What was I supposed to say to this guy? I started out slowly. "At the end of your life, what do you think you will regret?"

His eyes softened and he said quietly as if to himself, "All of it!"

"Wow," I replied as empathetically as I could manage. "Then what do you have to lose?"

He turned to me and said, "Everything and nothing, I guess." And that was that.

That conversation agitated me. The paradox of locking yourself out of your own future made my head swim. There is a real tragedy to being caught in that trap, too scared to lose if we make the wrong move, yet mired in unhappiness.

The optimist and the pessimist go for a walk with coffees in their hands. They round the corner and bump into a street person pushing a shopping cart filled with her life's possessions. Both quickly recover; as they walk on, the pessimist looks at the coffee spilled on his hands and clothing and says, "Look at this. I lost half my coffee here."

Meanwhile, the optimist looks back at the lady pushing her wobbly cart down the avenue and takes a moment to silently thank God for all that he is grateful for. He turns to the pessimist and says with a smile, "My cup is half full, would you like some?"

I later saw my new friend in the locker room, and I thanked him for trusting me with his truth. Uninvited I voiced my thoughts out loud, "I must be honest and tell you what I believe." He listened. "You should talk to some Holocaust survivors, people who suffered the worst injustices of mankind, those few who survived but lost absolutely everything; their families, careers, and all their possessions."

I took a breath.

"When they were liberated or came out of hiding, they had a choice to make about their futures. Some made their choice with a bullet, they could not live with themselves. Others chose to live in an angry, unforgiving state. But then there were others, among them the most successful, who with incredible courage made a choice to recreate themselves and their identities. To find new purpose; to love, live, and dance once again."

I let my comments sink in and I turned to him.

"At the end of the day, I have to completely disagree with you. We all have choices. We can choose to live unhappily and in regret or to take the risk to find our purpose and happiness."

I wish I could tell you this story had a happy ending, that this guy found his purpose. But as we get older, we can become more set in our ways and find it harder to climb out of the holes we find ourselves in. This man wanted to make changes, but not unless he knew for sure what he was getting into.

What he was missing was the understanding that he needed to give up control first, and then put himself out there. Here was someone who could help himself, yet it seemed that he was resigned to live the rest of his life with regret.

Making changes does not have to be all or nothing. Maybe, he starts off by making small changes, taking some risks, and giving faith and fate a chance. Doing things that give him purpose would serve to accelerate his confidence and give him the opportunity to visualize a more ideal future.

If you are younger and just beginning to make commitments in your life and career, consider this story carefully and be sure to ask yourself about whether the decisions you are making serve your sense of purpose. If you are older and have already made these decisions but feel like you lack purpose, it's never too late. Make the change. *If not now, when?* The future can still be bright.

Accelerators are the fuel for greatness. With every personal and professional project that we commit to and bring to the finish line, we increase the confidence we have in ourselves, the faith that others have in us, and our abilities to achieve larger tasks. But to open those doors, it starts with commitment. It starts with taking the shot. *Just do it!* as the famous ad campaign goes.

Mrs. Ellison, my grade five teacher, who at the time seemed older than God, would single me out because I did not have my lunch or because my work was not completed. She would hear no excuses. It did not matter to her that at ten years old, I had no one to make me lunch or that I would come to school in pretty bad shape. She would look me straight in the eye, a tremor in her voice, point a shaky finger at me, and say, "Young man, where there is a will, there is a way."

In retrospect, I have to thank her for her unwavering lack of empathy for me, even if the appropriate action might have been to call a children's aid society. She drummed that phrase into my head and it stuck. When I find myself in front of what appears to be an impenetrable wall, I recount her words, often saying them out loud in a chant-like fashion.

This mantra has kept me pushing and persevering over the years. There is always a way to move through walls. I have moved through many in my journey, and I will move through more. The commitment to moving through walls reminds me that by keeping stock in my faith and asking the universe to deliver, I will find that crack in the dam and a trickle of opportunity will make its way through to lead me to the next great place on my journey.

Challenging ourselves and pushing the boundaries of what we think we're capable of is a powerful accelerator. Accelerators related to physical endeavors can be particularly powerful. By persevering through physical discomfort, we learn to access new sources of confidence and motivation. Not to mention, it keeps you looking and feeling great, which is an accelerator all on its own!

When I am challenged in my home or work life, I recall moments like when I refused to give into my burning legs after intensely laboring up a mountain for over two hours, or when I navigated a 3-mile portage in a torrential downpour. I look back at past business success stories in my professional life, especially the scary ones where I took risks and played the odds. These moments have become ingrained in my psyche.

You do not have to be an athlete or a businessperson to experience these powerful moments. Think of a time in your personal life when you did something incredibly difficult and came out the other side. Each time you cross that finish line you are far stronger than you were before you started. When you need to find that next push, remember where you have been, and remind yourself that you will be able to move through that wall again. This is *acceleration*.

When I used to take on different projects or set myself goals, I wouldn't tell anyone. I would think: *If I tell someone about what I am doing and I don't get to the finish line, I'll look like an idiot.* I felt like I was just opening myself up to negative criticism. At some point, however, I started doing the opposite.

Including others in your creative process can be powerful. Talking about your ideas can help you further develop their details. The most insightful responses you receive may even come from random conversations you have with total strangers.

I've talked to myriad people about the idea of writing this book, and the result has been a work informed by a collection of views, some of which were outside of my own belief system. In many instances, my original thinking was challenged, and this influenced the final content.

An idea is not property; it doesn't belong to anyone until you deliver on it and unlock its potential. It was Mark Zuckerberg who delivered on the idea of a new social media idea called Facebook. Google founders Larry Page and Sergey Brin had an idea, a better way to surf the internet. Talking to people will strengthen your vision and help you on your journey of development. Either you will talk yourself out of the idea, or you will develop a vision that others will believe in, too.

If you have more than one project on the go at the same time, it's important to recognize when you are feeling overwhelmed and deal with that before it impedes you from bringing any of your efforts to completion. This is the risk of "negative traction." Life can throw barriers in your way without any warning.

When I was a teen, I would have lunch at this variety store that had a single arcade game, *Galaga*. For 25 cents you could be the captain of your own spaceship. Enemy strikers and asteroids would come at you with increasing speed. To survive, you had a limited supply of rockets to fire, and the ability to move to the right and left, ascend and descend. Now, when I find myself in triage mode, I visualize this game. I'm like: *Okay, throw whatever you got at me.*

There is actually very little that any one of us can do to totally avoid the unexpected and the unpredictable. There will always be events beyond our control. Ironically, the more you've got going on, the better you will be able to deal with the unexpected. Over time, I've become more restrained in my reactions to the unexpected. I swallow the panic rising in my throat, and instead try to break down the situation into its smallest pieces—until a solution surfaces. Sure, there are still days when I feel like things are coming at me from all sides, but I have learned to place trust in myself to make the adjustment and catch the wind.

Having a life-work balance is crucial for maintaining an optimal you. Dan Sullivan of Strategic Coach promotes a time management principle that involves dividing your days into three distinct categories: free days, focus days, and buffer days. The idea is that by managing your time this way you will optimize your energy, creativity, and motivation.

Focus days are all about focusing on your "unique abilities." These may be activities that serve your sense of purpose or are accelerators that bring you to a higher plane of confidence and performance. This is usually where your real value is.

Buffer days are for the necessary things that have to be done so that you can maintain your focus. Meetings, paperwork, admin, emails, research, etc., are activities that some of us may prefer to put off, but as they pile up, they can easily weigh us down and distract us from our focus. The idea is pretty simple: schedule the time to get things done that are important to your general maintenance. I usually take these days at my home office, where I am not easily distracted.

Free days are when you disconnect completely. Dan says that you should strive for 150 free days in a year. As a practicing Jew I have 52 Saturdays right off the bat, although I always laugh when I think of this joke:

> Sam approaches Mo in synagogue and says, "You know, Mo, if it weren't the holy Sabbath, I would tell you that my house is for sale." Mo replies, "You know, Sam, if it weren't the holy Sabbath, I would ask you how much." Sam replies, "You know, Mo, if it weren't the holy Sabbath, I would tell you that we would let it go at seven fifty."
>
> After services, Mo approaches Sam. "You know, Sam, I thought about it and if it weren't the holy Sabbath, I would offer you seven twenty." Sam replies, "Oh, Mo, if it weren't the

holy Sabbath, I would tell you that I already
shook on a deal with Harry for seven-forty."

There are more important things in life than the daily grind, and to achieve greatness you have to take care of the number-one person who makes things happen—you! By keeping on top of your buffer tasks and taking time for yourself, you will become far more powerful in your focus.

Ironically, distractions can sometimes be a good reset. Instead of following the compulsion to burn yourself out to meet deadlines, take some of that precious time off, and you may find that your ability to get to the finish line vastly improves.

As I write this book, I am actively involved in the operations of two distinctly different businesses, along with co-managing a family. That is a lot to keep track of! I have lists and lists of multiple tasks and finish lines I have to get to. Here is a little secret. *I sometimes play hooky.*

Remove yourself for an hour, day, week—even a month if you can do it. Distract yourself with an activity that has nothing to do with your "list." Temporarily disengaging yourself from tasks will leave you energized, rested, and more focused. When I occasionally remove myself, I allow my creative process to rejuvenate and to kick into a higher gear.

Being proactive and planning are important accelerators. When you mitigate risk through planned action, you create a sense of control that allows you to concentrate on looking forward to the next item on your list. Without a disciplined approach to everything I have going on, I'd be dead in the water, overcommitted and overwhelmed.

I've seen this kind of self-destruction happen all the time, especially when people take on too much without imposing a structure, and they implode. The challenge is to let go of your ego when this happens. It's time for openness and faith, not stubbornness and insistence.

I go through cycles where I have everything under control in one moment, and the very next moment I feel like everything is falling apart. When that happens, resetting becomes mission critical. Resetting can be as simple as sitting down and regrouping by going over all projects, sub-projects, and tasks. Break tasks down to their smallest parts and allow clarity to settle in, and the solutions will come to the surface. Focusing on the situation and gaining clarity on the variables provides empowerment, which brings back confidence and leads to actions that puts me back to where I can accelerate. Reverse the negative traction before it slows you down.

Pick projects to commit to that you can visualize finishing. Keeping focused on the projects that will provide the most value for your personal growth and build self-confidence are great accelerators.

When you're a highly creative person, coming up with ideas is no problem; your limiting factor is time. So, the first thing you need to do is realistically assess how long a project will take and whether you have the time resources to see it through. Don't commit to running a marathon if you know you only have an hour a week to train.

Be realistic about your relationship with structure and focus—a challenge for many highly creative people! It's also important to assess whether a project inspires you; there's no sense wasting time, money, or effort on something that doesn't. The litmus test I use is to answer three questions:

1. *Do I really believe in this?*

2. *Does this project give me purpose?*

3. *Is this something I am passionate about?*

Commit to projects for yourself, not others; don't do it because it sounds good, do it because you want to. Drive your actions through passions that speak to your purpose. You may not win the marathon, but that doesn't take away the fact that you finished what you started. Recognize your accomplishment for what it is, and then celebrate it!

Getting this book to the finish line has been a huge accelerator for me. From the original idea to the time of completion, I have invested over three years in this project. This endeavor answers my three motivation questions. I am excited to see where it takes me. *What projects can you do to create acceleration in your life?*

When we commit to something, give it our all, and see it through to the finish, the rewards are actually far greater than just a single moment of accomplishment. Accomplishments of every kind provide experiences that connect you to people who may forever change the course of your life. You may discover things about yourself that you did not know before. Strength and confidence grow with each positive achievement.

Using your purpose to generate power and moving from "strength to strength" is how you create your personal acceleration. Your life is happening now; don't be a bystander and simply let it pass you by.

Accelerators highlighted:

    1. Accelerators are positive achievements that propel you forward.

2. There are three stages to the evolution of an idea, from first thought to follow through: curiosity, consciousness, and commitment.

3. Prioritize and be stingy about what opportunities you pursue in order to safeguard your ability to reach the finish line.

4. Surround yourself with reminders of your accomplishments. These accelerators reaffirm your abilities and remind you that new stories can be made.

5. Each time you cross a finish line you are far stronger than you were before. When you need to find that next push, remember where you have been, and remind yourself that you will be able to move through that wall again.

6. An idea is not property; it doesn't belong to anyone until they deliver on it and unlock its potential. Either you will talk yourself out of the idea, or you will develop a vision that others will believe in, too.

7. Life-work balance is crucial for maintaining an optimal you. Don't forget to take care of number one—you! The ultimate goal is to make a living off your purpose and passion.

8. Commit to projects for yourself, not others. Let your actions be driven by passions that speak to your purpose.

Chapter Nine

FROM STRENGTH TO STRENGTH

Six Lessons

A man, as a general rule, owes very little to what he is born with — a man is what he makes of himself.

-Alexander Graham Bell

L earning from experience is a powerful part of the personal development process. We can choose to learn something from every event that happens in our lives. These lessons will guide us towards our destiny. In scientific experiments, researchers train mice to run through mazes using food as a motivator. Over time, the mice become faster and make fewer errors. The difference between the rodent and human experience is one of instinct versus choice. Mice do not possess the higher-level consciousness necessary to govern their learned behavior. We humans, however, can "choose" to learn from our past experiences. This is the gift of consciousness; how we use it is up to us.

Being mindful can help us to better understand our experiences and the reasons we make the choices we do. Learning from our experiences ideally prompts us to make better choices going forward. That said, certain painful events produce emotional and psychological interference that may prevent people from learning.

Let's return to the pain-pleasure pattern. On an unconscious level, it appears that when the levels of emotional intensity associated with a particular event are too high, it is incredibly difficult to learn from the event. The learning that may come from these traumatic events is a recognition of the subconscious triggers it embeds in us that cause us to make certain decisions. For the purpose of this discussion, however, I assume that we can learn from all our experiences—including lessons on how to overcome unhealthy emotional motivators.

Einstein's definition of insanity is doing the same thing over and over again expecting a different outcome. This is what the absence of learning and growth looks like: a mouse on a treadmill.

In this chapter, I am going to share with you six lessons that are based on wisdom I have gleaned from my personal history. The intent is that you may relate to these lessons, and then identify wisdom from your own experiences. When we learn from our experiences, we undergo a powerful personal awakening that strengthens us. My intent here is to illustrate how this strength can be leveraged to produce an even greater internal strength, one that will infuse all that we are and all that we do with new power and possibilities.

Lesson One: Put the "self" back in self-respect

I was inaugurated into our local synagogue's boys' choir and loyally attended practices every Thursday and Sunday from the age of six. The *chazzan* (cantor) was a classical performer, steeped in the traditional liturgy of Eastern European musical chanting. He was unfairly tough on me,[8] but he taught me to sing and to pray in a way that made my spirit soar. Today, when I have the opportunity to sing in this manner, it is a singularly focused experience; my mind empties and the incantation of the liturgy becomes my only conscious objective. For me, it is almost an out-of-body experience. I become one through the deliverance of song.

One evening when I was twelve, the cantor took his position at the podium in front of the assembled sections and announced that at the conclusion of the evening's practice the boy who had been with the choir the longest would receive a coveted solo with him in an upcoming concert. I looked around; that was me! I anticipated the announcement eagerly. But then, at the end of the practice, I was passed over and the solo was given to someone else.

The effect was instantaneous. I had reached a tipping point. Without even thinking about it, I went to the podium, and after several attempts to get the choirmaster's attention, he finally looked over at me as if I was interrupting something. "I just want you to know I cannot stay," I said. "I have to quit." With that, I turned on my heels and headed for the door. "Don't let the door kick you on the way out, kid" were his parting words. In that moment, I not only gave up the choir, but I lost the opportunity to sing at my own bar mitzvah, something I had looked forward to for many years.[9]

During my walk home, the fall wind bit into me, and any sense of pride I felt was overridden by the fear rising in my throat. "She" would not be happy. It turned out news had traveled fast, and as I predicted, it was not taken well. No sooner had I entered my home

---

[8] In 2011, I would co-produce a concert with my friend Jon Gasner to celebrate his career, bringing together 40 years of alumni for a one-time concert event.

[9] Actually, that opportunity was not lost; I sang the same duet with my sons Dov and Dean at their bar mitzvahs.

did a litany of abuse confront me, building from words into a physical frenzy. She could not believe that someone as worthless as me could or would defy her. The yelling and hitting went on well into the night, until I was left writhing on the floor to think about my actions.

Again, I felt myself reach a tipping point. I got up and slipped out of the house unnoticed. I walked farther than I had ever done before without anyone's permission. I ended up at a park a few miles away, where I sat on the edge of a hill and let out a fierce howl. I cried at my life and all its injustices. I asked the earth and trees in that dark, lonely moment why my life was the way it was, and then I sat in silence for hours hugging my bony legs tight to my shivering, bruised torso.

It was there, whilst licking my wounds, that the man in me started to emerge. Suddenly, I was filled with a powerful sense of self. For the first time in my life I had done something completely unexpected; I had stuck up for myself! I then experienced another empowering feeling, one that I struggled to identify. It was self-respect—and from that time forward, it was all I would need to defend myself against anyone who challenged me. That night, I had been pushed over a line, and I was not going back.

Two powerful things surfaced for me that day. One: I unleashed my self-respect. Taking control of my own life imbued me with a strength that I did not know I had. Two: I learned that I had the ability to draw the line when it comes to how people treat me. I discovered the agency within to withdraw license to those who believed they could take liberties to do with me as they wished.

When you do the unexpected, it alters the way others see you. When I slipped back into the house in the wee hours of the morning, my mother was sitting in a chair in the moonlit living room. I feared the worst. Instead, she called me over and kissed me. I can still feel her lips on my forehead some forty years later.

⌒⌒◯

When you look in the mirror, what do you see? Do you love that person? Do you respect that person? Self-respect is not about how the world sees you or an evaluation of your accomplishments but rather how you "choose" to see yourself. We all have within us the agency to create a strong sense of self and activate the power of self-respect through self-advocacy.

Practicing self-advocacy requires you to draw a line in the sand with regards to your relationships, forcing others to adjust how they treat you. If your relationships are built on strong foundations, they will survive a healthy level of self-respect. Self-advocacy is not always easy; don't underestimate the risk and courage it takes to assert yourself. If you don't speak for yourself, however, no one else will.

As a boy, I had to fight dark shadows at every moment, until one day thankfully I emerged into the light. I wanted to live, laugh, love, dance, and experience everything that a beautiful life had to offer. Gaining self-respect was the key to that transformation. The more respect you have for yourself, the less likely you will do things that disrespect yourself or allow others to disrespect you. And the more likely you are to find your greatness. Here are three questions I want you to consider:

1. *When I look at my reflection, what do I see and how do I feel?*

2. *What actions can I take—or not take—to increase my self-respect?*

3. *We give license to people to treat us in certain ways. How do the people around me make me feel? What am I doing to assert myself?*

Remember: You are worthy of respect, most importantly, your own respect. Live your life every day with the knowledge that you have earned and deserve the respect you have for yourself.

Lesson Two: Don't fight with pigs

Never Fight with a Pig (1991) is a book by Canadian entrepreneur Peter Thomas. I have a copy that was given to me by the man himself. I met Peter at a workshop for CEOs, where I was asked to speak about the future. One of the perks of being the founder of a cyber-technology company in the '90s was that it seemed to have qualified me as a futurist. After briefly meeting at the conference, Peter invited me for breakfast the next day, where he told me the story of how he founded, built, and eventually sold the real estate brokerage company Century 21. We met at the famed King Edward Hotel on King Street, where Peter had lived for 20 years after extending what was supposed to have been a one-night stay. Our breakfast took place August 28, 1995; the exact date is written on the inside cover of the signed book he gave me.

When I ran into some rough water with my VR company, Peter generously invited me to stay with him on his yacht, which was moored off North Vancouver. I remember that almost immediately after Peter welcomed me on board, he looked me straight in the eye and said, "I am happy to do this for you, but don't ask me for money." He said it in such a way that I was not taken aback; what stayed with me was his straightforward manner of talking—right to the point. He drew a line in the sand with total clarity.

In his book, Thomas imparts an important lesson and a timeless truth:

> Never fight with a pig—never allow yourself to lose sight of your goals and become involved in needless conflicts or hassles that provoke you. If winning will only help you "get even" or "show them who is right" then victory very likely simply isn't worth it. You can avoid most of the unpleasantness in business (and life) by avoiding conflict and the people who cause it.

I have thought about these words many times. They've helped me do the best thing I could do in some difficult situations: walk away. Do not do the predictable. Pigs will provoke you to get a reaction they desire. When you act unpredictably, you withdraw the power from your adversary. They become impotent. Doing absolutely nothing will frustrate the hell out of someone bent on engaging you. When a dog barks, do you bark back? A good example is road rage. People do things in an instant of rage to provoke a reaction, and the situation can escalate quite quickly. Do the unexpected: use restraint. Rob them of a reaction to their aggression.

I have met my share of pigs. Business is the natural habitat of people with self-serving ends, a great breeding ground for pigs, a place where it is easy to find a patch of mud to roll in!

When I realized that Gerry had stolen from our shared business, the disloyalty shook me to the core and sent me spiraling downwards. I took it very personally. It wasn't until I got on a plane to China to get back in control of the supply chain of products we were manufacturing that I started to recover. I used every practice I knew of to bring myself out from the bottom of that barrel—many of them are included in these pages.

I managed to depersonalize the incident and to get up and move forward. In fact, my rebound was so successful that if the dumb *schmuck* was honest, he could have pocketed profits totaling several times what he stole. Everyone who hears this story asks me the same questions, "Did you report him? Did you sue him?"

I cannot think of a clearer example of making the difficult commitment not to fight with a pig. Had I tried to bring him to task, I would not have been able to move forward. Instead I would have wallowed in the pain of having been deceived. I am not saying we should not use the legal system when wronged—that is what it is there for—but you have to consider the outcome and cost-benefit. I knew that it was unlikely I was going to recoup any of my losses, and I simply did not have time to play the victim; I needed to quickly get into recovery mode.

That momentum boost served me very well and helped me turn that dark year into one of my highest grossing years to that point. Looking back, it is clear that I got out of a toxic relationship at a very cheap price. Had I tried to fight with this pig, he would have dragged me further into the mud.

Ambition has a way of blinding intuition and encouraging greedy rationalizations. It can be easy to make compromising, short-term decisions. I learned that, no matter what the upside, the price you pay when you engage with a pig is just too high. I took Peter's words to heart and tried to be more honest with myself, let go of my ego and pride, keep my eye on the ball, and walk away when I had to.

At some point, we all need to take responsibility for the situations we find ourselves in and realize that toxic people create toxic situations and bad endings. As I like to say: "Shit comes from shit."

In business, this can be a hard lesson to live by. Looking back, I'm not proud of my associations with pigs, especially when I should have known better. I make no excuses nor do I carry any regrets. When you hunger to become something better and are driven by ambition, you cannot always be above compromising to gain a foothold. *But at what cost?* Achieving greatness requires learning how to recognize the pigs in our midst and not waiting for them to reveal themselves and consume us in never-ending conflicts that no one wins.

When you have identified who you are dealing with, the first thing you need to do is be accountable for having put yourself in a pen with a pig. Once you do that, figure out how the hell to get out. It won't be easy or painless, but the sooner you do it, the sooner the harm stops and the sooner you can move on.

Lesson Three: Talk to the rock

They say patience is a virtue, but the reality is that some situations may not lend themselves to a measured response.

The biblical Moses was appointed by God to lead the enslaved Israelites out of Egypt, and they trekked through the desert in search of the Promised Land. At some point, Moses complained to God that the people were thirsty. He was instructed to go to a rock and ask the rock to give forth water. Moses started to talk to the rock, but as he was doing this, the people became increasingly agitated and began to complain.

I can only imagine that moment: Moses, surrounded by an angry mob shouting, "Water, Water, We Want Water, Now!"

Parched and thirsty, slavery a distant memory, they were a demanding and ungrateful bunch. I would be quite rattled if 600,000 people were yelling at me. So, what did Moses do? He lost it. He raised his staff and he struck the rock.

Could you blame him? Remember the last time Moses lost his temper, he smote an Egyptian—which began his life on the run.[10] This time, water poured forth from the rock, enough to quench the thirst of the entire tribe of Israel, but God was angry. "You disobeyed me, Moses," he said. "I told you to talk to the rock—not hit it!" And then God revealed the devastating consequence: *No Promised Land for you, my friend.*

I think a lot about this scene. There are many times when personal frustration has led me to hit a rock. Each time, this reactive move has, so to speak, lost me the Promised Land. What am I doing when I hit that rock? I am giving in to what I see in front of me, and not trusting in myself, in my plan, or in my faith in what cannot be seen or touched. Being strategic is all about keeping the faith.

We all face a great deal of pressure when things start to go wrong. People shout at you. It's natural to start to lose your cool. But it is only when you give in to that reactive instinct, that things really unravel.

The lesson to be learned here is to keep your faith in what your plan is, and be patient as you guide your ship with confidence—don't push it and certainly don't lose it. Believe that you are part of this vast universe and *talk to the rock!* If you hit the rock you may still get results, but at what cost?

There have been more than a few times in my business career when I moved too quickly under pressure. When a group of investors put money into Cybermind's manufacturing division, we entered into a Letter of Intent and they waited until the last possible minute to pull out two books of legal agreements to sign. At that

---

[10] Compliments to my friend Miles E. Kuttler, from whom I have borrowed this sentence from his book: *Shabbat Greetings: Un-Orthodox Torah Thoughts for the 21st Century* (2017).

point, the money had already been allocated to product development and marketing projects. In our haste, we missed a critical point in those documents. That mistake would eventually cost me control of our flagship location at the CN Tower. In my haste and under pressure *I hit the rock.* You might ask: *Why didn't my lawyer see this?* Another lesson learned: *Don't cheap out on the expensive help.*

Years later, a very different scenario would unfold for me. AdvancePro needed capital, but I could not take the risk of ending up in a minority position. I kept to a strategy to create a win-win opportunity for everyone. I formed a plan, trusted my position, and patiently spoke to the rock. Many times, I could have walked away from the table in frustration, but I kept the endgame in mind and worked out a deal. In the end, I was able to protect my interests and come out on top. I succeeded in a potentially adversarial situation and managed to preserve my relationships—even with all the noise in the background. It confirmed what I had come to learn; trust in yourself, be patient with the process, and—whatever you do—don't hit the rock!

Lesson Four: Chew your food

Are you looking for motivation to start eating healthy? My suggestion is go sit in a Denny's in mid-country Any-town, USA. Just sit and watch what people order and how they eat. It's not just the excess of food; it's the way people literally shovel it into their mouths.

Here's the sad reality of a consumptive society: we strive for immediate pleasures and satisfactions. Happy to gratify those impulses are the same charlatans who used to pull their wagons into town and prey on unsuspecting villagers with games that were tilted inexorably in the house's favor. Only now, of course, they are huge multinational corporations. No free market opportunity has had such a detrimental effect on America's health than fast and cheap processed food. Our society has allowed the few to capitalize on the many by selling cheap, starchy, sugary, calorie-laden food coupled with a sentimental image of the best times had with Mom and Dad (before Dad has his coronary, of course).

I recently watched an advertisement for Zantac showing a good-looking healthy adult having a gastric attack from the fast food pizza he was eating. The ad's byline was: *Eat your way. Treat your way.* The message was: *Shovel as much crap as you want into your body, and take this pill!* We have reached a point where we no longer think about what we are putting into our mouths at all.

My grandmother used to caution me, "Slow down, *bubelah*, chew your food. It's not going anywhere." Well, Bubby knew a lot more than we gave her credit for. In fact, she may have been telling us something far more powerful. Our fast-paced lives tempt us to engage in a food-on-the-go lifestyle. Indeed, most of us have been guilty of fueling up on cheap fast foods.

I believe that mindful living starts with enhancing our consciousness around consumptive activities, like our food intake. Food, water, and air are the basis for life. The problem is that we have started to consume these things without making them part of a larger thought process. Growing up Jewish, I was taught to say a blessing before consuming food. Schools would compete in international contests that were based on knowing the specific blessing for different foods. It was like a spelling bee but for blessings.

Recognizing what is before you and saying a prayer specific to this nourishment makes you stop and think for a moment. Two things arise from this. One, you realize that neither you, nor anyone else, is necessarily entitled to have this food. It is a gift. Two, the food in front of you is a miracle.

If we think about all that has to happen for food to make it to our tables, it is truly miraculous; it is the proverbial *manna* from heaven that sustains us. Acknowledgement of our food is a very important practice. *What should possibly give us more faith than the availability of food in our lives?* Just ask anyone who has gone hungry, and I am sure they will back me up on this.

Acknowledgement of this gift is truly humbling. So, *chew your food.* Don't shovel it in; think about it and be mindful. If you do, you are likely to become mindful of just about everything else in your life.

Lesson Five: Move through walls

At various points in our lives, it is inevitable that we are going to hit a wall. Sometimes, we will hit it hard. These proverbial walls are places in which we encounter a sense of impossibility. There may seem to be no way forward. A sense of helplessness and panic can easily set in.

I have written about the choices we face when we hit a wall. Some people may simply choose to sit down and watch as the wall soars higher and higher above. Then they get up, shrug their shoulders, turn around, and go back to where they came from. Others choose to confront the wall and move through it. *Which person are you?*

The ability to move through that wall depends on the approach you take: the way you perceive the situation, the manner in which you think about it, and your attitude. If you see a wall in front of you, and you want to get to the other side, what do you do? *Climb it, right?*

As we are dealing with a metaphor here, let's agree to look at the wall differently. Sit back for a moment and visualize the wall. Place your hands on it and imagine that where you make contact, the surface dissolves with your touch. This is the first step. However, while you can visualize just about anything, it is the power of your own conscious intention that will move you through that wall. You must, however, be willing and committed to do so. Concentrate on your intent, and allow the solution to come into focus. Finding a solution starts with a strong faith and belief that the solution will present itself in the exact moment it needs to.

I was on the twenty-third floor of a friend's condo in downtown Vancouver when for a few scary moments everything physical seemed to liquefy. It was the strangest experience. The walls shuddered; what seemed solid only seconds before changed form in an instant. When it stopped, we realized we had been through an earthquake.

In that moment, I was reminded that what we think we know is not necessarily true or real or definite. Walls are not permanent; we are just conditioned to see them as such. Yes, it is counterintuitive to look at a wall and think: *I am going to move through that.* But that is the point. Thinking and acting against conventional notions and ingrained beliefs has got me to the other side of that wall on many occasions.

There are, of course, walls that seem higher than others; for example, personal tragedies can throw up barriers that seem insurmountable. In 2015, Cheryl Sandberg (COO of Facebook) suddenly and tragically lost her husband, David, in a freak occurrence while on vacation. Overnight, she became a single parent and sole provider without the partner she had believed would be present for their journey together. She co-wrote a candid book called *Option B* (2017) with Adam Grant about her experiences.

In it, she describes how she moved through the walls that result from losing someone you deeply love and suddenly having your life thrown into chaos. She quotes psychologist Martin Seligman's three P's, factors that can interfere with people's recovery from tragic events: personalization, pervasiveness, and permanence.

The idea that we tend to blame ourselves for something that happened beyond our control is "personalization." The idea that what has happened will affect everything that we do is "pervasiveness." Thinking that things will never be the same, "the belief that the aftershocks of the event will last forever," is "permanence."

When my father in-law died from brain cancer in 1998, none of us could see much of a future, especially my mother in-law—who struggled badly for a number of years before she found a way through that wall. Fifteen years later, we found ourselves adrift with the tragic untimely passing of my mother-in-law. Once again we were left with this incredible void in our lives.

Moving through a wall does not mean that the void is no longer felt. The loss is still there. What it does mean is that you can accept and believe in a future beyond that wall. Sandberg sums it up well: "We all deal with loss: jobs lost, loves lost, lives lost. The question is not whether these things will happen. They will, and we will have to face them." Resilience, she writes, is "finding the hope to love and laugh again when love is cruelly taken from you. And finding a way to hang onto love even when the person you love is gone."

I have been moving through walls every day for as long as I can remember. In business, and in life, any number of unpredictable events come up on a daily basis. Triaging solutions is a part of leadership. Over the years, I have learned to take a step back and manage anything that comes my way using a measured approach. I only need to remind myself of my many past positive achievements to know with confidence that I can overcome and move through that wall once again. I use my personal experiences as my arsenal.

When we have the opportunity to confront and overcome a challenge, there is a tipping point in the process, a decisive moment when your inner strength emerges. Remember that moment and take it out when you need to remind yourself that you can do this again.

Sometimes you may need to create a wall in order to summon your inner strength. Coming through to the other side of "whatever" can be very rewarding. I very much appreciated the story of Cheryl Strayed, the author of *Wild* (2012). After losing her mother and looking at her life, she felt she needed to do something drastic to shake up her destructive path. Her solution was to hike the Pacific Crest Trail, a 2,650-mile trail running from Southern California to Northern British Columbia. Along the way, she encountered both literal and figurative walls that forced her to think about her life, and ultimately enabled her to come to a fuller understanding of who she is.

Pushing past my own limits has always inspired me. Surpassing self-imposed walls has helped me to gain greater clarity around my own goals and abilities. When I hit those walls, a new strength emerges that I was not aware of prior. Pushing through the walls creates its own momentum; it helps us become stronger and stronger—and move from strength to strength.

Some of my most memorable times have been the survival trips I took with my friends Howard and Brian. A five-day trip down the Des Moines River with nothing but what we could hump through the wilderness provided us with many challenges, facing the elements and seemingly isolated from the rest of the world. Putting up a tent in the pouring rain and mud, or hunting three miles downstream for gear after tipping my canoe, challenged my resilience. There were moments when I would simply hit the wall. Coming through the other side filled me with a strength and a resolve that I could package and compartmentalize within to use in entirely different situations.

I made it through that wall then, I will make it through this wall now.

Over his three years of service in the Golani brigade, my son Eitan has hit many walls in the *shetach* (field). When he tells me his stories, I say, "Eitan, seize that moment for your future."

Capture that feeling, place it in a box, and bring it out when you need it.

Lesson Six: Misadventures caused by assumptions

Most of our assumptions have outlived their uselessness.

-Marshall McLuhan

When we make assumptions about the wealth of someone else, we reveal a lot about ourselves. I am not talking about a passing moment of appreciation for someone's fancy toys, but rather thinking too hard about what another person has and how you might leverage that to your advantage. The golden rule is: *Don't look in someone else's pocket.* To expend effort thinking about what other people are banking will always distract you from playing the long game. Applying subjective impressions of someone during the deal-making process will only hurt the deal and negatively impact your negotiating skills.

I will admit to pulling out my mental calculator in a packed venue, multiplying the number of seats by the price of admission, and musing at the intake; however, this is not what I am referring to here. Assumptions about people you are in business with can cloud your judgment and lead you to misjudge the situation. If you think someone doesn't have money, you are liable to low-ball a deal because you feel bad. If you think someone does have money, you might high-ball the deal and lose out altogether.

This idea not only applies in business; it also has an impact on our personal and social lives. Strive to accept people as they are. Don't focus on your own assumptions, because these guesses will impact the relationship. Real, long-standing relationships are about acceptance and love—without conditions.

> *I am your friend because of the person you are and the values and beliefs we share. I am your friend because of how you make me feel. I respect you for you.*

When I walk into someone's beautiful home, I wish them happiness and communicate this clearly: *Your home is so beautiful, and you have such an opportunity to do so many good things.* I celebrate their good fortune. I am truly happy for their success.

Being content is a great multiplier of our sense of self-worth. Being compared to, or comparing yourself to, others is self-depreciating. Enough is never enough, there will always be someone who has more. There is a parable about a man who was told that he would receive all the land he could manage to cover on foot in one day. The man ran and ran, loath to pass up the opportunity to acquire one more acre, one more yard. When he could run no longer, he crawled. As he finally collapsed from exhaustion, he stretched out his hands, straining to cover yet another few inches. "This, too, is mine" were his dying words.

Have confidence in the value you bring to the table. And consider what value you place on the person sitting across from you. Initial impressions are surface optics. *We are taught from an early age not to judge a book by its cover, but we often do, don't we?*

It's human nature to see the world as a reflection of how we see and feel about ourselves. The impressions we have of others are rooted in our own belief systems. Therefore, it's best to monitor our own biases and figure out what we really believe, before making judgments.

———

Optics aside, our first impressions can also be influenced by plain gossip. Gossip serves no positive purpose and we should guard ourselves against it because it will surely drag us away from finding greatness.

Israel Meir Kagan (1838–1933) was a respected Talmudist and ethicist admired by all people who came to know him. He was called the *Chofetz Chaim* (desirer of life) after the title of his first book (1873), which had the same name and was directed against the evils of slander and malicious gossip.

> *What is he that delights in life and love many days that he may see good? Keep your tongue from evil, and your lips from speaking guile.*
>
> *-Psalms 34:13–14*

The venerable rabbi staked his career on bringing awareness to the ills of gossip, which he considered to be the most harmful and decisive force in humankind. He taught that when you speak ill of someone else, you kill three people: the person who is being discussed, the person who is listening, and the person who is talking.

The tendency to focus on surface issues is amplified in a consumer-driven society obsessed with optics. Social media has put even greater value on eye candy while providing the means to make judgments on a far wider scale. The same technologies have amplified the "fake news" phenomenon. I find it interesting that there is such a continuous rush to judgment on so many vital issues based on such limited and sometimes unbelievable information!

Assumptions may be benign at times, but collectively can easily cloud our general judgment and weaken our communal bonds. A great deal of damage can come from confusing our assumptions with reality.

In the discussion on openness in Chapter Two, I discussed the concept and dangers that can arrive from confirmation bias—which plays quite well with the idea of collective assumption forming around a particular issue. I often marvel at the baseless claims voiced by relatively intelligent people as a result of some wave of popular group-think. The Liberal ideology has shifted so far to the right today that I have to look to my left to find the conservatives.

Assumptions arise from two places: our emotions and our imagination. When making decisions, my strategy is to remove as much emotion as possible and consider my options and choices from an objective and researched perspective. I can't do that when someone is "selling" me. The pressure of the sale is counter to the art of the sale, which should be focused on hitting all the appropriate emotional buttons. During business debriefs I often ask presenters to please remove descriptive phrasing. I don't want to be pulled into their emotional traps and I want to see if they have real information to share underneath the fancy packaging. "Just the facts, please," I say. If they persist, the meeting is over.

Don't mistake the emotional decision-making process that is external to you and damaging to good decision making with your internal intuitive response. When we react to surface images or savvy advertising we can make ill-informed choices. We submit to collective reasoning based on the environmental factors and societal norms, rather than on truth and fact.

Intuition is a visceral response that is all about the innate decision-making process. Usually, it's the first thought or feeling about a situation—not emotionally produced or intelligently deduced. The intuitive response leverages personal balance and self-confidence. As we become healthier and closer to our optimal selves, the quality of our intuitive decision making improves dramatically. Filter for subjective bias, but don't second guess your first thoughts; they are usually on the mark.

The judgments we make come from our subjective consciousness. When people do not conform to our positions, we can actually "feel" resentful and betrayed. The truth is, our emotions can produce infantile reactions to unmet expectations that everyone will agree with us all the time. To be great, we need to strive for objectivity, and that means countering our natural tendency to become so committed to our own assumptions that we cannot tolerate other viewpoints.

I don't recall living in a more sensitive time to discuss political thought. Trump-ism may be the topic of conversation that has created the greatest divide. The Liberal left's view has dominated, leaving anyone with an alternative opinion feeling intimidated and outcast. The comparisons by intelligent people that are coming off the public news feed today are so off the mark that it's scary, and is nominally an affront to actual historical events. Populism is running rampant on both sides of the political spectrum, at the cost of reason.

The early twentieth century was a rich period for the study of human psychology. The Freudian era produced the venerable psychologist Erich Fromm (1900–1980), whose books focus on the human psyche. In *The Art of Loving* (1956), Fromm asserts that narcissism is at the opposite pole of objectivity. The ability to move past the narcissistic mind set "is the faculty to see other people and things *as they are*, objectively, and to be able to separate this *objective* picture from a picture which is formed by one's desires and fears."

Fromm argues that humility is a prerequisite for objectivity. The stubbornness that prevents us from letting go of our belief system to open ourselves up to new possibilities is the product of our ego, the home of our self-centered selves. Humility is the essential prerequisite to override the ego and access reason. To quote Fromm:

> To be objective, to use one's reason, is possible only if one has achieved an attitude of humility, if one has emerged from the dreams of omniscience and omnipotence which one has as a child. Love, being dependent on the relative absence of narcissism, requires the development of humility, objectivity and reason. I must try to see the difference between *my* picture of a person and his behavior, as it is narcissistically distorted, and the person's reality as it exists regardless of my interests, needs and fears.

We can often consciously seek the truth beyond our assumptions by asking a simple question: *How do I know this?* Instead of starting from a place of certainty and defensiveness, start with an open mind and heart. Initiate a conversation. Learn where a person is coming from. Ask questions for clarity, until you can form an objective opinion. You will never get the real and right answer without asking.

How often do we wish in retrospect that we could turn back the clock? Four things can happen in your personal and professional life when you jump to judgment based on mistaken assumptions:

- Missed opportunities
- Errors in judgment and therefore actions
- Overconfidence
- Misunderstanding people

The wrong assumptions will limit your opportunity to be great because your actions will be based on a biased perception of the situation. Don't make this mistake.

When we enter situations and relationships with an open and positive manner, we can understand them objectively and thereby make decisions based on reality, rather than preconceived notions. This will lead us to where we are meant to be. Our destination is our destiny; to arrive there, our actions must be powered by openness, faith, a strong sense of our future, and the ability to forgive. This is how greatness is achieved.

Chapter Ten

SELF-WORTH

All You Need Is Love

There is a Hassidic story. A pupil sees his rabbi in a sad mood and asks him, "Master, why are you sad? Are you sad that you have not reached the highest knowledge, that you have not the greatest virtues?" The master said, "No, I am not sad about that. I am sad not to have become myself totally." That is to say, in every human being there is an optimum of what he could become, there are things that he could never become. So many people waste their life by trying to become what they could not be and by neglecting to be what they could become. So a person in the first place should have a certain image of what he could and what could not become, what are the limitations and what are the possibilities.

-From an interview with Erich Fromm, with Gerard Khoury (1980)[11]

As I approached my 51st birthday, I experienced an intense feeling of anxiety and began to question my relevancy. *What was my usefulness to the world? Had I made my mark?* I looked

---

[11] This interview was conducted 14 days before Erich Fromm died.

around and noticed I was not alone. I was joined by not just people in their mid-lives, but young people trying to figure out their place in the world. It occurred to me that we are all vulnerable to how we view ourselves, and this can be destabilizing when we lack the answers to important questions. I could clearly see that there was one more chapter to write, perhaps the most important one, on how we value ourselves.

Loving yourself, as I will discuss in some detail here, is foundational to your sense of self-worth. After all, the only relevancy that matters is that of feeling relevant to yourself. Indeed, loving yourself is a precursor to everything we have discussed in this book. It's because you love yourself and recognize your value that you can open yourself beyond bias, have faith in that which you cannot control, believe in a future, and forgive—depersonalize, empathize, and move on. Without self-love there remains a wanting that will distract you from the depth of understanding yourself in the world you live.

But sometimes loving ourselves isn't easy. We can be our own worst enemies, complicating our lives with anxieties about all the things we cannot control. We doubt our own intent and worry too much about what others think. We exist in a pleasure-pain circle fueled by the ongoing collection of personal injustices.

> *I try to grab hold of something that will stop my fall. Fear tightens its grip and my breathing becomes labored. My focus is erratic; I must find the calm. I am looking for a bottom but below me is an endless abyss.*

Life can start to go wrong very quickly, and when that happens, a momentum can build that if left unchecked can create a negative slide in you and your emotions. No one is immune to reactive triggers, but to honor our future we must do everything we can to ascend back to an optimal place of being. Time to shut off the auto pilot and get back into the game!

Recognizing a bad place may not be enough to counter our instinctual, reactive, emotional responses while we are in the midst of it. However, if we have the presence of mind to recognize our heightened emotional responsiveness, we can limit our emotional turmoil and negative momentum from building.

In these pages, I have identified practices that can be used as tools to build awareness and to stop the spiral of depreciation. In fact, these practices can slingshot you to a better place than where you were initially, bringing you to an even higher level of functioning and creativity.

> *Observe, be mindful. Breathe. Take stock of your positive achievements. Announce out loud and recognize all the gifts you have received. Be grateful. Step back and stop trying to control. Have faith. Believe that there is an amazing future around the corner. You are loved. Live in the moment.*

Self-worth comes from knowing yourself. The founder of Taoism, Chinese philosopher Lao-Tzu (6th century BC), is quoted as stating: "If you live in the past you'll be depressed, if you're always thinking about the future you'll be anxious, but if you learn to live in the moment, you'll be true."

Focusing on the past can cause us to compare our present with how things used to be or to second guess the decisions we have made and the path we have taken. In either case, this type of contemplation leads nowhere. We cannot change what has already happened, so we are left feeling powerless. Believing you have a future is good; obsessing about it isn't. There is no crystal ball, but there is faith; we cannot know what is going to be but we can articulate what we need to happen.

It is important to remember that ultimately *we are not in control*. But the most powerful lesson here is that by living in the present, we can unlock an understanding of our "true" selves. The actions we take in the moment reveal us to ourselves.

Living in the moment is one way to learn to know yourself and thereby build your sense of self-worth. After all, life is ultimately the sum of all the moments in the present, and in between those moments are the choices we make. We do not live life in a vacuum. Other people shape our present and our decisions. I may be a product of my own personality, but I have to give credit to all those who have influenced me and shaped my thinking along the way.

According to the psychiatrist Herbert Sullivan (1892–1949), it is our interpersonal relationships that strongly influence our personality development and self-understanding. Sullivan believed that "one's personality did not reside within an inner self but in the interpersonal field—in a social environment with other people. Individual personality was the pattern of recurrent interpersonal encounters, real and imagined, which characterized one's life."[12]

In other words, you are who you associate with. I agree that our personalities, and to some extent our values, are the product of our close interpersonal relationships, but ultimately these associations are often choices we make and reflect what we want for our future. Over the course of my own journey, I sought the mentorship of people who were kind and charitable enough to become my teachers and friends, and who helped shaped who I would become.

My self-awareness has also been shaped by the many books I read and from the understanding I found within their pages. Bergler, Fromm, and Frankl, among other writers and thinkers,

---

[12] From *The Lives of Erich Fromm*, Lawrence Freidman, 2013, p.85

were my guides. Observing and having the privilege to get to know people who survived the Holocaust has had a profound influence in my life. They are people who define the very essence of the word *resilience.*

If they could survive, how can I not?

My wife's grandfather, Eliasz, was a man who needed no one to approve of him. Content in his very being. He found joy in everything. He treated all people as equals and deserving of his kindness and attention. He understood his worth despite surviving events that eroded humanity. As the years went by, I found myself outgrowing some of my living mentors—but never him.

I see many of the interactions and connections we make in life as steps we take in our journey. Some connections may not last, but we can remain grateful for what we learned. It is healthy for relationships to intertwine throughout life; I often find myself reconnecting with people I had lost touch with. I think the relationships we choose to be a part of say a lot about us, but to really come to know ourselves and be true to ourselves, it is necessary to carve out our own independence.

I can see the independence of my own children growing as they chart their life course. The ability to establish their own identities is fundamental to them developing a sense of self-worth. I marvel at these four precious gifts in my life, and am so proud of each of them. In turn, they have strengthened me beyond any words I can write.

I believe that the extent to which you are able to effectively transform, actualize, and optimize your life relates directly to your sense of self-worth. How you value yourself is internally generated. It's the "you" in you, representative of your intrinsic values and unique qualities. Self-worth can be measured in terms of your self-understanding, self-love, and self-acceptance. These are the internal qualities that survive once everything external is stripped away.

This externally dependent sense of self is the "esteem" we think and feel about ourselves, which is based on cues we get from the outside world. These cues can include our physical appearance or our material acquisitions. Our relevancy to the world around us is important for being able to fit into the social expectations of our community—but feeling relevant is not the same as valuing ourselves.

The people you are surrounded by, the nature of your profession, your material worth, and your personal appearance may contribute to your self-esteem, but they are not intrinsic to your real self-worth. You may feel good about the outside you, but still not feel deserving of love because you do not feel worthy. Your self-esteem can be healthy, while your self-worth is not. That said, the two can have a symbiotic relationship and feed into each other.

The quality of the external factors in our lives—relationships, profession, and money—are a direct reflection of our sense of self-worth. A sense of self-worth is key to the people you attract and are involved with. Self-esteem may be a reflection of self-worth in part, but if we become too preoccupied by externalities, they can have a negative impact on our sense of self-worth.

If your self-esteem has been driving your sense of self-worth during the good times, it can be a rough ride in times of turbulence. The world around you should have less effect on your being than your being has on the world around you. When you have a strong sense of self-worth, no matter what happens, you are in no danger of losing who you are.

It took me some time to understand that attaching my sense of worth to external factors in my life had depreciating effects. The visual that comes to mind is an artichoke. Peeling away the petals—all those surface layers and desires—to get to the heart—

the real truth. After her father died, Limore and I promised ourselves that we would invest our time in only worthwhile and meaningful relationships. We wanted more substance in our lives, more value. At first, we did not know what this would look like, but it felt important to focus on the things and people that fed our "true selves," not our self-esteem or status in the world. We were humbled by tragedies and wanted the world to mean more for us.

Humility is a key trait to building a sense of self-worth. As your need for approval by other people and dependency on external factors lessens, you become more free to pursue and nurture your self-worth.

As I was coming of age, hungering for a healthy and successful future, I had to confront a critical inner voice shaped by years of painful childhood experiences. I grew up being told terrible things about myself. Silencing that voice was critical to my ability to build a healthier self. I will always be grateful to the few who recognized my value and potential when I did not, and gave me snippets of encouragement—which were like drips of water to a parched wanderer lost in the desert. Finding my sense of self-value allowed me to stand up and withdraw the license that gave some the liberty to depreciate me.

Faith, belief, and love are foundational to building self-worth. *How do you perceive yourself? How do you describe yourself when talking to others? Do you belittle your worth and make light of your talents, or do you exaggerate your qualities?* People exist along a spectrum that ranges from self-effacing to egotistical and arrogant. Not presenting yourself in the best possible light should not be mistaken for humility; over-emphasizing your abilities should not be mistaken for confidence. Greatness is about confidence in the knowledge that you are valuable and vulnerable, unique and worthy, and humble and grateful.

Today, people of all ages, genders, and backgrounds face significant challenges to their sense of self. Thanks to the unprecedented advances in communication and information, we now invite constant comparison and judgment from others into our lives—and face pressure to conform. The challenge is to focus on being who you really are, being true to you.

If you find yourself worried about how you are being perceived, switch the narrative and become aware of how you make yourself feel. Avoid living for others at the expense of yourself. If you feel compromised, then you know you're not in a healthy situation. The secret is to listen and trust yourself. It's not about what others say; it's about listening to the truth down deep inside and adjusting your beliefs and actions to align with your sense of value.

Now ask yourself the questions again: *How do you perceive yourself? How do you describe yourself when talking to others? Do you belittle your worth and make light of your talents, or do you exaggerate your qualities?*

Self-understanding, self-love, and self-acceptance are the keys to becoming your truest self. Each of these will bring balance and authenticity to your life. By seeking to understand the true you, loving the true you, and accepting the true you, you will make choices that will result in you achieving the greatest you and the life you want.

When I was 24, I drove a brand-spanking new Oldsmobile Calais coupe. It was loaded to the nines, and when I drove it, I felt great. Then one day, having not been able to make the lease payments, I had to give the car back. It was devastating and made me feel like a failure. My not-yet father-in-law, being the great guy he was, sent me to a mechanic buddy of his to pick up a rusted older model Chevy Camaro. I'll never forget the night I picked it up. There were layers of dog hair everywhere and the car smelled.

When I arrived at their house, Dov put his huge hands on my shoulders and said in his thick Israeli accent, "Don't worry; we will fix her up like new."

At that moment I almost lost it. Driving home, I thought about my reaction and it weighed heavily on me. *What kind of person am I?* I thought. *Is my value really all about the car I drive?*

Over time, that Camaro would became a symbol to me that happiness wasn't a fancy fast car I couldn't afford. The experience became an opportunity to understand my truer self. I was stirred by the gratefulness I started to feel just to have a car, thanks to the generosity of someone who didn't owe me anything.

Dov, true to his word, had the car fixed up, beautifully restored in fire engine red.

Self-understanding is not about asking the question: *Who am I?* but rather *What motivates me?* Is it a bigger house, a better car, the envy of your colleagues, pretty photos on Facebook? Because if it is, I think you will find, as I did, that changes of fortune will have an outsized effect on your sense of self-value.

Try to imagine yourself without material possessions, naked like the first people in the Garden of Eden. *What's important to you now? What inspires you? Do you like the person you see?*

Self-understanding requires us to look beyond our possessions and our egos to see what lies beneath it all. Only when we can truly see ourselves, can we believe in our value.

～～

Self-love draws a line between what inspires you and what diminishes you. Loving yourself goes far deeper than purely surface appearances. It is about looking after yourself on every level—physically, spiritually, and psychologically. A healthy feeling of love fosters a positive inner energy that acts as a catalyst for positive relationships. Love equates to valuing and respecting yourself and others.

A deficit in self-love has the potential to have damaging effects on your person. There are some very valid nature-nurture debates about the causes of addiction, but it is clear that people suffering from an addiction are hurting deeply inside.

While a person's tendency towards addiction may very well be out of their control, what often triggers the addiction may include situations involving peer pressure or an immense loneliness, in which people feel so unloved and unwanted they lose the ability to love themselves.

Addiction is not only about substance abuse, but can also easily include engaging in self-damaging behaviors and other associations. This damage is exacerbated by the pain-pleasure pattern: unconsciously desiring and finding pleasure in further pain, thereby increasing the damage to ourselves.

One powerful way out of this cycle is unconditional love. Earlier on, I talked about the need to forgive in order to free up the mental space and energy needed for creative output. Allowing yourself to forgive is an act of self-love. When you are secure in the love you have for yourself, you stop allowing others' actions, opinions, and judgments affect your inner balance and potentially cause a chain reaction of self-doubt and negative behavior. Forgiving yourself and treating yourself with kindness, generosity, tolerance, and compassion are all essential to self-love.

No rock unturned. I can move past disappointments by recognizing the reality that I cannot control everything. There is a tipping point where I will say to myself, "I have truly done all that I could. What happens now is my destiny."

To build self-worth, we must be real with ourselves. We are not perfect beings, and we do not need to make excuses for who we are. What we do need to do is to take responsibility. People get into trouble when they conduct their lives according to other people's ideas. Accepting your unique self is powerful currency.

People who live their lives in conflict with who they really are will eventually run up against their own truth. For some, this way of life is a conscious choice, made because of specific circumstances or in service of a life vision to which they are dedicated. For others, it is a default position, and they find themselves straddling the fence between what others expect of them and what they really want to be, unable to live fully in either world.

Existing with a delta between the life you live and your "truth" is going to lessen your sense of self-value over time. The resulting regret usually plays out in frustration released at yourself and others.

Living your life in harmony with your unique self is going to result in a positive momentum and produce greater feelings of self-worth. The more truthful you are to yourself, the more currency you have to spend finding your greatness. Acceptance starts with "you" accepting "you." No one else's judgment or acceptance of you is more important than your own.

Not too long ago, I bumped into an old friend of mine, and in updating each other she told me that for the first time in 25 years, she was off to do something entirely for herself. "My husband and kids can fend for themselves," she went on. "I am going away to build a house!" She revealed that she was taking part in a Habitat for Humanity project.

Wow! I thought to myself later—her idea of doing something for herself was to do something for others. What a beautiful intersection of her higher purpose with her sense of self-value! Through her actions, she was topping up her personal currency, which in turn optimizes her personal and professional life. Indeed, the decisions we make about how we live is directly related to our sense of self-worth.

If there is one thing I took away from my intro to economics class at university, it was the idea of having to "choose" between competing things, both of which are limited and finite. This struck me as an important life lesson, and I quickly realized that one of the commodities in life that is completely limited and finite is my time. If I choose to do one thing, it costs me the opportunity to do another. This means that each decision, each action, has a price to it. You can make the choice to invest your time in doing something that pays long-term dividends at the cost of immediate gratification, or vice versa. Like everything else, balance is important—taking stock of how you are spending your time will make you more conscious and mindful about the decisions you make.

At the end of your days, you will be able to look in the rear view mirror of life and be the ultimate judge of how you have spent your time. It's either going to be a moment marked by joy and gratefulness, or one filled with regret and sorrow. If you can imagine the latter, it's not too late; change your life starting right now. If there is one guarantee in life, it's that you will never be able to turn back time and play it again. Making good choices in how you spend your time will create personal value. Be greedy with your time.

It is easy to get distracted by the many choices now available to us in our fast-moving world. The multitude of professions we can pursue, the places we can live, the media we can choose to consume, and the people we can meet and commit to. With an unprecedented wealth of choices at our doorstep, it's no wonder that people find themselves frozen in fear at the thought of missing out. FOMO (fear of missing out) is an anxiety disorder in this day and age. It leaves people wondering what they missed out on and causes them to lose out on the present. Worse, it can create a continual state of indecision.

The cure to FOMO is simple. When you love yourself and fill yourself with conscious gratitude, you will be content with wherever the universe has dropped you off and your feelings of missing out will disappear.

Ernest Hemingway was once challenged to tell a story in six words. He came up with the famous six-word story: "For Sale: Baby shoes, never worn." Inspired by this story, Larry Smith of *SMITH Magazine* challenged others to try to write their lives in six words.

I thought this idea was quite the challenge. *How could you encapsulate a life in six words?* I was struck by both the brilliant simplicity and the enormity of the challenge: sum up the total sense of who I am and what I believe and package it in a six-word micro-memoir.

I was stumped. For several days, I considered what impact these six words would have on how I value myself. Six words does not allow for any excess; it requires the writer to focus in on what is most important. The exercise took on a new challenge for me. I realized it was asking me to distill my life down to my core essential truth.

When I eventually committed my six words to paper, I felt a great wave of relief come over me. I was calmed by its truth: *Living my Life on my Terms.* In six words, I captured the feeling of the gratefulness I felt and how far I'd come to understand what a gift life is. Every time I see these words they continue to strengthen and inspire me.

Try it yourself. *What are your six words?* Facing your real six words can be very revealing and therapeutic, and once you have committed them to paper, they become a tangible reflection of yourself. My friend Randall Craig shared with me two of his: *The next chapter is even better*, and *I am in charge of me*. Both very powerful statements.

At the end of a close game, my younger son's hockey coach turned to him and said, "When you have the puck, don't hold onto it. Take the shot!" There is a deep and complex relationship between our sense of self-worth and the actions we take. In the software business, we essentially sell change. But change can be fearful territory for any business, even one convinced of the benefits. This hesitation can be a significant psychological barrier to moving forward.

Often in life, we are faced with moments where we need to take that shot, but find ourselves second guessing, doubting, or simply uncertain about making the commitment, and therefore are unable to take important risks that could be a game changer in our life. The more impactful the decision, the harder it becomes to make. *What school should I go to? What profession should I pursue? What investments should I make? Should I marry/leave him/her? Should I start this new business venture? Should I sell the family home?* The number of decisions, large and small, that we face can be endless.

Our confidence in making decisions is driven by our sense of worth; this is what determines the belief we have in ourselves. In turn, that belief stems from our acceptance and love of our real selves. All of these things come together to make up our personal currency, which ultimately underwrites all the actions we take in our life.

Success can happen in the flash of a moment, or at the end of a long game of strategy and planning. Our ability to identify and take advantage of opportunity hinges on the health of our intuitive abilities. Have you ever watched a close-up of a lizard as its tongue extends in an instant to eat its prey? It occurs almost faster than the human eye can comprehend. That visual says something about seizing opportunity—the lizard is not pondering "should I do this?" or "maybe I'll miss?" He has a very small window of opportunity; if he pondered, even for a millisecond, he would starve.

Looking back, it has been my faith in my intuition that has allowed me to identify moments of opportunity. It has been the confidence I gained in my abilities and staying power that prepared me for moments of opportunity that I had faith would present themselves. It is these types of moments that I can attribute my successes to.

When success happens, it is the sum total value of who you are in the moment that will prepare you to take the shot. I came across a great quote credited to Oprah that sums it up nicely: "Luck is a matter of preparation meeting opportunity."

I love myself and I'm okay with the possibility that I can make a mistake. The people closest to me are also okay with that.

Regret only occurs when you have not done everything within your power to succeed. It is a sign of failure. I have never known something good not to come from the momentum of following through on a vision with everything I have. Success may not look the way you first envisioned it, but as long as you put your best self forward, you will succeed. The tools you put to work—openness, faith, future, forgiveness—will ensure success because they lead to self-love and self-respect, not failure. They will help you find pleasure in what is good for you, not in what causes you pain. When you use these tools, you can never fail. There are no wrong moves, and as such, you have nothing to fear but fear itself.

When someone suffers from indecision, it is a sign that fear is taking over. Indecisiveness indicates a loss of self-confidence and results from being out of balance with the universe. It occurs when someone does not have faith, but rather is trying to control the people and world around them. Spinning into reactiveness, they find themselves questioning every move.

Extreme indecision is a state of feeling overwhelmed by the consequences of decisions; in this state, it is hard to figure out whether to go right or left at an intersection. Even the most minor decisions—*What should I have for breakfast?*—require inner debate. A person suffering from indecision wants to know the right answer, the outcome, but because they don't have a crystal ball, they are paralyzed, caught up in passive spiraling, helpless to act. Like a plane stalled and in a death dive, they desperately need to pull up. In this state, even when a decision is made, the approach is manic and aggressive, and rarely leads to the positive result necessary to stop this negative momentum.

We all have moments of indecision. Sometimes this occurs because there is no clear-cut answer; other times, we are emotionally connected—too close to the situation and its outcomes—to make a decision. Indecision can be a sign of an emotional breakdown. I have been faced with tough decisions in extremely stressful times. The red light flashes in my head: *Pull up, pull up!*

In these moments, it is important to know when to step back and ask for help. Finding someone good to talk things through with will bring clarity to the surface. Not being able to articulate the anxiety you feel causes that death stall. It is important to identify the source of issues, and you'll soon be back to taking confident decisive actions.

Have you ever sat down at a restaurant and been unable to make a decision? You read the menu like a novel, page by page, as if hoping for divine inspiration. Then, there's that delightful dinner companion who asks about this or that, makes a decision, reverses the decision, and finally asks the waiter to return in a minute. These are minor instances of indecision—we all have them—but the ramifications can still be serious. Being indecisive draws us into a reactive state, where we are easily overwhelmed and can find ourselves stuck. Decisions are tough because they force us to face the fact that when we make a choice, we do so at the cost of other options. *No wonder combo platters are so popular!*

Indecision can be easily related to FOMO and a lack of confidence in the face of the unknown. Indecision can be countered by visualizing what you want, and then going for it. The trick is to not get sidetracked with all the options.

Avoid indecision by taking a meditative moment and visualizing the outcome in advance. Simply *(but it's not always simple, is it?)* ask yourself: *What do I want?* Making that decision in your mind ahead of time, before being distracted by a list of options, can help you be decisive. Getting in touch with what you want, no matter how large or small it is, is the key to avoiding indecision and slipping into reactive living.

The choices we make are ultimately a reflection of how we see the world, framed by our beliefs. Objectivity comes from an inner sense of self-value and confidence in our intuitive process. When we allow others to make our decisions, or are dependent on the approval of others, our sense of self diminishes.

An emotionally healthy person with a strong sense of self-worth will possess a healthy intuition. A strong sense of self-value will give you the confidence to trust your intuition; this in turn increases your decision-making ability.

It is actually entirely possible for all of us to make the best choices every day of our lives. Stay open to the universe and all its secrets. Have faith in yourself and others. Believe in a positive future ahead for you in every moment. Practice forgiveness—don't harbor anger. Focus on positive achievements. Power your confidence by loving and accepting yourself, and being true to yourself.

Listen to your intuition because believing in yourself means less double guessing. You've got the puck lined up—the only thing left to do now is *take the shot*!

How do I measure myself?

Most of us like to think of ourselves as unique, and yet we get caught up in conforming with social and cultural norms. It is easy to see ourselves reflected through the eyes of others and become preoccupied by how we think others see us. Our physical appearance, our sense of fashion, even our actions are shaped by a society that tells us how we "should" look, dress, and act. Most of us want to fit in with our peers—and finding commonalities with others is not always a negative.

The problem occurs when we place more importance on these externalities than on our own purpose, truth, and values. *What's the right balance between honoring our individualities and fitting in with the community we choose to associate with?* Unfortunately, there's no clear-cut answer. Being an outsider is not always fun; there can be enjoyment and comfort in adhering to a set of "norms." On the other hand, to what extent are we willing to compromise our real selves to fit in?

Consider these five personal metrics: appearance, bank account, social circle, career, and achievements. *How much do these "external" factors—by themselves or combined—contribute to your overall sense of worth and well-being? A lot? A little?* This question is important because giving too much weight to things that are beyond our control is a risk to our self-worth.

Having external factors drive our self-worth ill-prepares us for unexpected losses and unmet expectations. Your house, car, clothes, waist size—these may certainly contribute to your sense of self-esteem, but when these things become central to your sense of self-worth, they produce a cycle of endless wanting, making happiness and self-satisfaction illusive.

Think back to the questions I posed earlier: *If you were stripped of everything, would you still know who you were? Would you still have value?*

How do I feel about me?

Feelings can be both simple and complex. Simple feelings tend to be short term and tied to involuntary physical reactions mediated by the autonomic nervous system. Complex feelings last longer, and are linked to our thought and image processing centers. Both types of feelings can emerge from and interact with our overriding emotional state. For example, if we are in a state of feeling positive and confident, we are more likely to experience feelings of joy, anticipation, and trust.

It is possible to experience several feelings at the same time. Our feelings are usually a derivative of our thoughts, perceptions, and attitudes. If you are an injustice collector, you are more likely to be on the negative spectrum of feelings, whereas if you are prone to giving people the benefit of the doubt, you are more likely to be on the positive spectrum and experience positive feelings. A "cup half full" attitude will certainly create more positive feelings than a "cup half empty" attitude.

Feelings create their own kind of energy and can be contagious. Hang out with positive, healthy people and you are likely to "catch" some of their positive emotions. When you are feeling strong, creative, confident, grateful, and happy, you will infect others with your positive sense of self and attract others of the same ilk. This attraction makes for powerful opportunities and for optimal relationships. Of course, when you are in a negative emotional state, the opposite can happen.

Feelings can have physiological effects. For example, they can provoke panic attacks, trembling, and excessive sweating. From the time I was a small boy and well into my early twenties, I was plagued with severe stomach pain, which was commonly diagnosed as IBS, a generic term for *we don't know what this is.* As I started to experience positive healthy emotional growth, the symptoms became less acute, and the severe gastric attacks less frequent.

In the process of becoming more in tune with yourself, don't be surprised if your body provides the first and strongest indication of your newfound sense of self.

Many who know me have heard my "there are no rules" speech. Those who suppress true feelings—either because they feel guilt or because they come from a place where expression is not encouraged—are at a disadvantage when working to achieve their potential.

When it comes to feelings, there is no right or wrong. It is important to "allow" the feelings we experience to freely surface. What we "feel" is the mechanism that helps us through disappointment and pain, and pushes us towards taking action with our lives. Talking out how you feel will give voice to your true feelings and frame them in the context of the reality of your life. This can be very powerful in self-understanding and actualization.

Harness the power of openness and faith while developing ownership of your personal narrative. A good listener will help guide you to a greater and clearer understanding of your feelings. When listening to people, I love the *a-ha* moment when the question asked leads to the clarity desired. In that moment, we hit the nail on the head.

Journaling is a great way to express your feelings. I've talked about how visceral exercises make things very real. The act of writing clarifies and codifies existing feelings. Reviewing what you have written can be quite revealing. A release of feelings is a healthy emotional liberation. Bottle something up and eventually the pressure will cause it to explode.

When my mother died, I could not cry. Not when I was told. Not at the funeral. Not during the *shiva*. I thought I "should" cry. *What kind of person does not cry for their own mother?* Then suddenly, months later, randomly, this incredible overwhelming feeling overcame me. I was alone. I started to heave, shaking and crying—I could not stop myself and I didn't want to.

When these moments come upon you, let them happen. These spontaneous incidents are your body's way of releasing the pent-up emotions that need to be discharged. Do yourself a favor and when those moments overtake you, allow yourself to cry, to curse, to sing, to dance. This is part of loving yourself without restrictions.

How we feel about ourselves will often correlate with the life we choose to live. When our feelings are in conflict with our lifestyle, which in turn often intersects with our belief systems, depreciating complexities can surface that may affect our sense of self-worth, and by extension our opportunities for being optimal. If this happens, a choice must be made to make a change that will increase our positive feelings about ourselves.

Change is not always easy; it requires strength and self-confidence, tenacity, and perseverance. A strong sense of self-worth is imperative; it fuels the sort of healthy intuition necessary to make the correct changes and to see us through the process. Some changes will be obvious; others may take years to understand and to undertake the course of action necessary. Actualizing change has everything to do with how we feel about ourselves.

In calculating how you feel about yourself, answer honestly: *Am I a happy person? Do I walk the world upright? Are my feelings in sync with my lifestyle? Community? My friends? Am I grateful?* The stronger and more confident you feel about yourself overall, the greater your life will become in every way.

Do I love?

Measuring the love you feel for yourself, and by extension for others, is integral to your calculation of self-worth. Visualize a vertical line from 0 to 5. The more love you have in your life, the higher your score. A high score indicates we feel love for ourselves, love for others, and are feeling loved. A low score indicates we find it difficult to feel love for others because we do not love ourselves enough. *What's your score?*

Feeling good about yourself is about loving yourself. Self-love was given a bad rap in early twentieth-century thinking. Freud saw love as a manifestation of the libido; an expression of self-love, it was believed, indicated a selfish person who only loved himself and therefore could not love others. Self-love was mistaken for narcissistic imbalance.

Fromm departed significantly from Freud, claiming that not to love yourself is to not love. In his view, self-love and selfishness are at opposite ends of the spectrum. A selfish person may appear to be someone who loves themselves too much, and thereby lacks compassion and empathy for others. But Fromm argues it's the contrary. Such a person does not suffer from a surfeit of love, but from the pain of being separated from love. He or she is selfish precisely because they do not love themselves. The more selfish a person is, the more in pain they are in, and the less able they are to love themselves. Selfishness is a state of unhappiness where a person finds themselves cut off from everyone—including themselves.

The flipside of selfishness would be selflessness, and these two personalities may have more in common than you would think—both being the extreme ends of the spectrum. Someone who appears to be completely selfless and who always puts the interests and care of others first, before themselves, is likely to be someone who is failing to feel and extend love.

While the altruism may seem commendable to others, it often masks inner turmoil. That selflessness may be coming from a place of extreme unhappiness and could suggest a person who does not feel they are worthy of being loved and therefore is incapable of loving. Extremely selfless people are typically sad because they are missing out on giving love to the one person who needs them most—themselves.

If you are one of these people, take care of yourself; recognize *your* feelings, achieve *your* dreams, give back to *yourself*—you will not be a healthy influence on others until you can take these steps. Taking care of your needs is most important when it comes to giving to others.

In his book *The Art of Loving* (1956), Fromm contends that "love" is the "mainstream" of all psychology: "Even if we knew a thousand times more of ourselves, we would never reach the bottom. The only way of full knowledge (of ourselves) lies in the *act* of love."

Fromm's clinical practices differed greatly from conventional practices of the day. He strongly believed that he had to share himself to understand his subject; that empathy was essential in the analytical and healing relationship. He did away with the couch tradition of psychoanalysis and preferred his patients to sit and make eye contact with him. Fromm worked at humanizing the process by fostering interpersonal relationships based on equality and unconditional love.

Fromm quoted the Bible to support his notions:

> Love thy neighbor as thyself implies that respect for one's own integrity and uniqueness, love for and understanding of one's own self, cannot be separated from respect and love and understanding for another individual. The love for my own self is inseparably connected with the love for any other being.[13]

The ability to love others is rooted in the ability to love ourselves. And the extent to which we love ourselves depends on the positive feelings we have about our own selves.

There is a spectrum along which co-dependence and full loving exist. At one end of the spectrum is co-dependency. Here is a person whose love for others is rooted in co-dependent relationships, causing them to love themselves less.

These relationships are often seen as "wanting" because one person in the love equation may feel the weight of neediness of the other person too strongly. Let us assume that one person is completely devoted and selfless, and is therefore hurt to feel that their love is not being reciprocated; the dependency becomes a countervailing force to the relationship. However, as the individual becomes more self-assured and starts to love and do more for themselves, the relationship changes; the co-dependency lessens, and the trueness of love can emerge. Once in a healthy place, the couple's growth together is once again possible.

For years, you may find yourself providing the very sustenance needed for existence and survival. How easy it must be to lose yourself in this role of selfless provider and forget to find time and find love for yourself.

---

[13] Ibid., p. 54.

By the time I came along, my mother hadn't had a moment to herself in six years. She had given everything she had to the point that she had forgotten how to give back to herself. Exhausted by the demands placed on her to love and take care of new babies arriving every year since the beginning of her marriage, she felt unloved in a world where there was no outlet for her emotions or an independent existence. She became separated from herself. Trapped in a marriage that was not what she had dreamed of, she had forgotten what it was to love herself, and thus became unable to love and deal with life in a healthy, balanced way.

It was very powerful for me to come to this realization, this understanding of her world. When we can truly empathize with someone else's story, it is much easier to depersonalize and forgive. What went on in my home was extremely complex, and no child should be subjected to the kind of abuse I experienced. There is no excuse. But I have found some degree of understanding, and with this, some peace.

So long as you are dependent upon and obligated to love and care for others more than yourself, you will be drained until you have nothing more to give. Often, this tends to coincide with a growing degree of discontent and unhappiness. It is only when the love you give to yourself is at minimum equal to the love you give to others, that your sense of your own value will prosper, and new avenues of opportunity will present themselves.

Man is gifted with reason; he is life being aware of itself; he has awareness of himself, of his fellow man, of his past, and of the possibilities of his future.

-Erich Fromm, The Art of Loving

The measurement of your worth will affect the kind of life you will live. Put simply, to be happy and satisfied with the person who you have become will give you the ultimate sense of peace while navigating the peaks and valleys of life. You will believe in yourself regardless of what has been, where you are, and what you will become.

I dedicated an entire chapter of this book to the subject of *future*. Seeing a future for yourself is perhaps most essential to self-awareness, and is foundational to every choice we make. *What are we without hope?* Our dreams light the path ahead. Seeing a future for yourself and being able to clearly articulate the plan to reach it is what makes achieving greatness possible. Being your best requires you to see the light at the end of the tunnel, in addition to being able to imagine the expanse of opportunities for happiness, love, and purpose.

Self-worth highlighted:
1. Self-worth comes from knowing and loving yourself.
2. Self-worth can be measured in terms of our self-understanding, self-love, and self-acceptance. These are internal qualities that survive once everything external is stripped away.
3. Attaching our sense of worth to external factors in life can have depreciating effects, especially if the things that we depend on for that feeling fall away.
4. To build self-worth, we must be real with ourselves. The more truthful we are to ourselves, the more currency we have to spend finding our greatness.
5. Success may not look the way we first envisioned it, but as long as we put our best self forward, we will always succeed.
6. Line yourself up for the opportunities that will come your way. Take the shot! You can only make the shots you take.

For every ending there is a beginning

UNLEASH YOUR GREATNESS

Those who have a WHY to live can bear with almost any HOW.

-Viktor Frankl

A chieving greatness starts with an innate desire to take full advantage of the life you have been given. That desire spawns the dreams we have of who we want to be and what we want to achieve. To become reality, these dreams cannot be vague or aspirational; they must be textured and detailed visualizations of what we want our future to become, like an architectural plan that lays out precisely what we wish to build.

And it's not enough for us to wish for what we want; we have to make our wants into needs. Wants are like tasty, but unsubstantial delicacies, while needs are the actual sustenance that feeds our being; only one of these will give us the fuel to build our best life.

If there's one thing that I've found in the course of my life and career, it's that people are terribly frightened to dream of what could be their best lives. Many simply won't do it, which is such a waste. Because at the end of the day, we are what we believe about ourselves. A visiting friend commented to me, "You walk around like you own the place." And I thought: *Why not?* If we wish to become our greatest iteration, that begins with achieving an open understanding of, and daring to visualize, what that actually is.

When we stop dreaming, we start accepting the status quo. We begin preferring the illusion of security to the risk of change, and when we do this, the potential to reach our personal best drifts away, out into the blackness of the universe, beyond reach. Personal greatness is not a natural state or a right we're born with; we can only achieve it by actively striving for it and making it happen.

Our greatness is not about how others see us—it's not 15 minutes of fame and fortune—rather, it's about how we see, accept, and love ourselves. Think about that: the only thing standing between you and your greatness is you. That's it. There is nothing stopping you from employing the tools I have discussed in this book and starting to live your life in a more meaningful way, now, today.

At any moment—at this moment—you can start down the path to becoming your greatest self. You can dream and plan, and breathe life into, the future you want. Once you do this, your actions and patterns of behavior will reinforce each other, driving you every day to new heights—until living with greatness eventually becomes instinctive and natural.

Don't worry about what you need to do to achieve greatness; if you embrace openness and have faith, the "how" will be revealed. Focus on your end-game goal, your future, and everything else will happen as it needs to. Dare yourself to dream and believe that you can move through every wall along the way. This is the path to your greatness.

On the eve of his 90th birthday, seated at the head of the dining room table, surrounded by his family, I followed the gaze of Eliasz as he took in each person. It felt like he was taking a snapshot, freezing the moment in time. He seemed content and resolved. There was a serenity about him, a real peace.

I believe now that in that moment he was not reflecting on his own end, but rather on all the new beginnings he had played a part in creating. A legacy that had been built not on some dumb luck but rather on his fierce effort and determination, bolstered by a fundamental, unshakeable belief in himself and the gift of life itself. His was the ultimate triumph over evil. I hoped that one day I too would be deserving of a similarly powerful moment.

But we don't need to wait until our 90th birthdays to truly be present in the moment and appreciate what is before us. We can endeavor to do this in every moment; we can choose at any time to look around and see the culmination of our hard work in ourselves and the people we have touched and been touched by in our life. We can be content, even as we strive for a vision of the future, because everything we've done has led us to this moment. Our shared history is the launching pad to who we want to become and where we want to be in the future.

I met a man at a dinner party who was lamenting the death of a contemporary. He described the many accomplishments of the deceased man, who was an immigrant like himself, and how he had amassed extraordinary wealth, only to suddenly drop dead of a cardiac arrest.

"Without warning," my dinner party companion said. "One day he is serving up drinks and celebrating with his friends, and the next day he is done."

He continued, "None of his wealth or achievements could save him; they make no difference in the end."

He paused and then said, "What a wake-up call, eh?"

I thought out loud, "Why wait for a wake-up call? Wake up every day." Every day we have the choice and opportunity to wake up to the fact that life is both unpredictably limited and a limitless gift. This clarity allows for the realization that we can influence the events of our day and that we get to decide whether we spend it celebrating the greatness we have achieved or wallowing in regret for what could have been. I have said it already, but it's worth restating:

We are born and we will die, it's the choices we make and what we do in between that defines us. Don't settle for the status quo: make your life a journey unlike any other, where each day is unexpected and leads you to heights you've never been before.

In the social milieu we live in, it can be hard to resist the pulls of popular movements and trends. We are constantly being influenced by mainstream thought and told what we should want and desire, which may influence our perspective—even without our knowing it. It is easy to get caught up in consumerist narratives that are devoid of purpose. Tune in to your inner voice and inner belief in your vision of your future. Know what you believe in, and be courageous in following your truth.

There are times when your truth may conflict with more "popular" ideas or beliefs, and people may try to dismiss or decry it. Let them. Don't give in to the path of least resistance or follow the masses. Do not wait for history to tell your story in retrospect and weigh in on what should have been or could have been your life.

This lack of purposeful direction leads to regret because it shows that you haven't listened to yourself, nor have you used your time to pursue your purpose. Lead with what you believe. Be proactive and create your own story—make it one of greatness!

Beware of people who will denigrate your dreams and self-belief out of a sense of their own personal dissatisfaction with life. Make conscious choices about the people you invest your energy and time in. We can easily become who we surround ourselves with. When we choose to be involved in negative relationships that make us feel bad about ourselves, we put up a wall between us and our potential. This wall is a potentially toxic choice we have made, and we need to recognize what we are getting out of that choice. We also need to recognize why we—too often—experience pleasure from this pain we create. Only when we can clear these self-imposed blockages can we truly begin to be open to the possibilities around us.

Life is a gift, and we get to choose what we do with that gift. We can neglect it and take it for granted, or we can recognize what an incredible privilege we have been given and try to honor it through our decisions and actions. We can think of ourselves as the center around which everything else revolves, and align our purpose accordingly (which will lead to a focus on consuming and taking), or we can think of ourselves as part of a much larger circle and let that perspective inform our purpose (which will lead to a focus on giving).

I discussed the value of eudemonic versus hedonomic living, as well as studies that suggest that practicing the former leads to a longer and more fulfilled life. As with everything else in life, balance is key. Life can contain a healthy amount of giving as well as taking; taking one or the other to the extreme is bound to offset the balance, and when you are out of balance it is much easier to trip and fall.

Each of us has the capacity to be our best selves, but what is greatness? Personal greatness might look different for each of us— this is the beauty of the diversity of life, that which makes each of us unique and individual—but regardless of what it looks like, your greatness is always within reach. *So what's stopping you from achieving it? Everything has to start somewhere, so why not here and now?*

The journey to your greatness can start with something as simple as grabbing a pen and paper and mapping out a vision for your future. It can start with taking that one step towards the unknown that you have found every excuse under the sun not to take. Or by giving yourself the gift of loving yourself enough to forgive and release the past; depersonalizing and empathizing to remove the sense of injustice that has been holding you back. Or, it can start with consciously identifying the physical reaction that occurs when your ego is challenged and by opening yourself up to extending the benefit of the doubt, letting go of your bias, and considering your own subjectivity with objectiveness.

Shifting from being reactive to being proactive can start with a single prayer of gratefulness. Consider out loud all that you have received so you can create that important shift, and thereby reverse the downward spiral. Invite your shadow to share your space. Recognize openly where you have come from, and be responsible and accountable to yourself for where you are going.

We are all born with the power of choice; we can choose to wake up and take action. The best part of pursuing your greatest self is that the momentum builds naturally, and the success you experience will breed more success.

If you've read this far in this book, you possess the hunger to become great. The positive rituals you adopt will turn into habits and subsequently become a new way of life. The practices I have written about will bring alignment to your focus so you can catch that positive momentum. All that's left for you to do is to make the conscious commitment to listen to yourself and take action!

In this book, I have discussed the Berglerian premise that our actions and behaviors, which in turn determine our outcomes, are driven by unconscious motivators that seek the most obvious and natural reward: pleasure. Unlike other creatures, we have the ability to make conscious choices instead of being governed by instincts we have no control over.

The salmon instinctively swims upstream, even though in doing so, it ensures its own death. In contrast, we can choose to change the course of our lives simply by recognizing that our actions are based on seeking pleasure and then understanding what it is that we are taking pleasure from. (I do not permit alternative rationalizations for actions and behaviors because doing so would open the door for people to make excuses for not becoming the best person they can be.) If we take pleasure from putting ourselves in positions that hurt us, we will choose relationships, participate in behaviors, and take actions that cause us pain. All of this negativity will compile to ensure that we never achieve our personal greatness!

So, how do we rewire our responses so that we no longer find pleasure in pain? Our emotional responses are determined by our subconscious selves, which can make it very difficult to change them. The first step is to become aware of these responses; when we do, we can start seeing them for what they are and then questioning them. This recognition will allow us to make choices consciously and objectively, rather than subconsciously and subjectively. The effect can be transformative.

A healthy intuition is nourished by receiving pleasure from pleasure, not pleasure from pain. So is creativity; as the walls the subconscious set up come down, ideas start to flow. During this process, it can help us to surround ourselves with the right people, people who bring to light new ideas and breed confidence and further creativity. It can help us to stop injustice collecting and start tuning into the universe, where all our needs can become reality. Being accountable for the pain you are experiencing by recognizing that it originates from the choices you make is in itself very powerful. But when you practice openness and have faith and make this admission out loud by saying, "I am here because of the choices I have made, which have come from a deeply rooted subconscious desire to receive pleasure from the pain I am ultimately responsible for causing"—it is absolutely magical what happens next.

Almost instantly—simply by saying these words and believing them—the unconscious link between pleasure and pain is broken. You start taking pleasure in pleasure, and things stop going wrong. If you get one thing out of this book, take this away with you. It is one of the keys to unlocking your greatness. Place it in the keyhole and turn. It's that simple.

While I truly believe that positive momentum will build on your journey, it will not always be easy. There will be people who hurt you. Projects that fail. There are going to be rejections and times when things do not work out. That is the way life goes. You can't change it. But it is within your power to prevent these negative events from gaining hold and putting you into a reactive place.

My first name "Israel" roughly translates to "he who has struggled with God and overcame."[14] I could not have been more aptly named. I believe we all face struggles and that struggles are ultimately good. It is when people stop struggling that they become complacent and, in some cases, indifferent, going through the motions rather than creating a path forward. Without struggle, we could not become who we are meant to be.

---

[14] In the Bible, Jacob is renamed Israel after his struggle with an angel.

When we struggle we are actively searching for a higher meaning, and the resistance we face can lead us to a mindful state where we can clearly see and act on the intentions and purpose that drives us. No one wants their life to be like that tree that falls in the forest without being heard, but not everyone has the courage to struggle and strive for their own greatness.

Think of these struggles as a gift. Becoming your greatest self is about recognizing when life throws you a curve ball, you can use your positive beliefs and actions to get right back on track and move forward—feeling capable, creative, productive, fulfilled, and alive.

Remember this: not succeeding is not the same as failure; not doing everything in your power to succeed is failure. Commit to the four foundational principles discussed in this book and observe the magic that happens. The returns are huge when you practice openness, commit to having faith, visualize your future, and allow yourself to forgive. With these principles in hand, you will move through walls and find greatness within your grasp. You will wake up.

The challenges and struggles we face are actually very brief windows of opportunity. They commonly appear when least expected, and work in mysterious ways. Don't fight them or ignore them; listen to your intuitive voice when they arise; it will often tell you something you don't yet know. Our challenges and struggles are gifts; take them seriously and allow them to lead you to where you need to be.

I have hopefully inspired you to begin or to renew your journey towards personal greatness, and want to I leave you with these final thoughts.

Always remember that the energy you project outwards will determine how others react to you and treat you. This energy is directly related to how you feel about yourself. Your sense of self-worth is so material to how you treat yourself and, by extension, the license you give to others when it comes to how they treat you.

That sense of self-worth can be built through self-examination, acting in accordance with what gives you purpose, taking on and achieving positive accelerators, and practicing mindfulness. The simple act of smiling can pay huge dividends, building positive energy both within yourself and in your interactions with others. Saying a prayer of gratefulness can completely alter your energy, and that positivity will project out into the world. Fill yourself with love, and recognize out loud the respect you have for the people you encounter. That message and feeling will resonate and ultimately return back to you multiplied.

Kick-start your faith to magnify your sense of power and place in the universe. Take the words of the ancient Maimonides who said, "I believe with all my heart" that the Messiah would come. You are your own Messiah—you are coming to deliver you! Believe with all your heart. Go all in! This will empower you to give up control and put your faith in a higher power.

If you put your best foot forward and do everything within your power, you will come to a place that is your destiny. "Believe" that you are loved. "Believe" that you have value. And "believe" that you are an important part of this vast universe, one that is a far better place because you have chosen to pursue your greatness, and in doing so, have affected the world in ways that you may never become aware of.

Stay true to your purpose. When people's questions make you feel defensive or make you question yourself, it's a sign that you are invested in their approval, which indicates an emotional lack or void in your psyche. Do not let people cause you to self-depreciate. If you are acting in synergy with what gives you purpose, it is much easier to stay committed and strong, and to move forward with confidence, no matter what people say or how they choose to judge you.

Take the time to explore your purpose, and make decisions, think of new ideas, and consider relationships in the context of your purpose. You are an explorer, the captain of your own ship, navigating your life. The wind is at your back, filling up the sails as you head into the horizon of your future. Keep your eyes forward and don't get distracted; your purpose will guide you to where you need to be.

What I have to say in this book speaks to you because you are either already in a place where you hunger for greatness or because something I have said has clicked with you. As you move through the walls that threaten to stop your advancement and you follow your path to greatness, you will want to share your insights with people you know and people you meet. This is natural.

Finding your greatness is exciting and life-changing; it also connects you to a sense of giving and gratitude. Through this process, many of us will find that one of our purposes is to share what we've learned with others. I love the way my son Dean loves to share a piece of whatever delicious treat he has found: "*Aba* (Dad), here have a bite." When we enjoy something or think it might help others, we have a very human need to share it with someone else. This impulse comes from a positive place; we want to do good for others and bring them the joy we feel.

For this reason, it can be frustrating to find that not everyone is ready to listen to what we have to say or wants to change their lives for the better, and there is very little we can do to change that. People's behaviors and actions are driven by their own purpose and intent. We cannot give someone else purpose. We cannot make them commit to a different set of behaviors or course of action.

Everyone must discover what they want out of life, what gives them purpose, for themselves. It's hard to stand by and watch someone we love self-destruct, but at the end of the day, the only thing we can do is set an example and provide encouragement. Don't get discouraged by other people's attitudes or choices; they do not determine your path or your future. You do.

Stay mindful. While the hunger to succeed and change is an important part of turning your dreams into reality, you must be careful never to let it overpower mindfully living in the moment and being grateful for what you have today. As I said earlier, the seeds of the future are planted today. A reactive and negative mindset, and an inability to see and appreciate the gifts we have today, will keep us focused on the past and the injustices we've experienced, rather than on our purpose and the opportunities we will encounter while moving forward. Being content in the moment allows us to tune in, look up, drop our biases, and create the future we want—one where we can be our greatest selves.

And finally, don't be afraid. We are not in control, and that's okay. I used to torture myself with existential questions: *Does life happen to me? Or do I make life happen? Do I have control, or am I controlled by forces larger than me?* What I've come to understand is that the answer to all these questions is: *Yes.* I have allowed myself to adopt a belief in a higher power, which gives me great comfort, but I operate with the knowledge that only through my actions and beliefs can I put myself in a position where I can tap into the workings of that higher power to pave the way to where I need to be. During my most stressful moments, I remind myself out loud:

> *I am doing everything I can do, I can only do what I can do, and the outcome will be what it will be. Knowing I have done my best, I can accept this.*

With this mantra, I affirm that there is a master plan and that I am a part of it. That there is only so much I can control and then I have to let go. This thinking removes noise and gives me the best shot at attracting the answers and people I seek at the right time.

Looking forward, the universe seems unpredictable, but when we look back, everything seems to fit and to have happened as it was meant to. Trust in your future. Make every minute count. And don't be shy about wanting to be your best self. It's the path less traveled, and making that commitment can make all the difference. Let me know how it turns out!

Acknowledgements

I owe a great deal of gratitude to those I have studied, who have helped me to articulate the ideas I have put forth here. I hope I have given the credit due to these thinkers who have brought my whispers to a shout. Their contributions to human thought, especially now, have given a gift to so many of us who have sought to put a complicated world into perspective.

My children: Arielle, Eitan, Dov, and Dean. They are probably unaware of how much they have helped to heal the boy inside the man. Watching them grow into healthy loving people is by far my greatest triumph.

Limore is my wife, my partner, and my friend. I am so grateful for her; she embodies the saying: *Behind every man is a greater woman.*

To Kathryn Willms, who believed in this project and helped me broaden the appeal of my ideas. To my friend Randall Craig who gave me the encouragement to start this journey and without hesitation agreed to be the first to read this manuscript and provide me with his mentorship.

I also dedicate this book to you, the reader. You will turn the page because you value the gift of life you have been given, and if I can touch your life then I have succeeded in my efforts.

To all those who have been there for me throughout my journey, I can only say thank you for giving me what I cannot repay. Your unconditional friendship, love, and support has been life-changing.

CPSIA information can be obtained
at www.ICGtesting.com
Printed in the USA
BVHW071930240119
538631BV00001B/8/P